Editor-in-Chief and Founder:
Lyndon H. LaRouche, Jr.
Editorial Board: *Lyndon H. LaRouche, Jr. , Helga Zepp-LaRouche, Paul Gallagher, Tony Papert, Gerald Rose, Dennis Small, Jeffrey Steinberg, William Wertz*
Co-Editors: *Paul Gallagher, Tony Papert*
Managing Editor: *Nancy Spannaus*
Technology: *Marsha Freeman*
Books: *Katherine Notley*
Ebooks: *Richard Burden*
Graphics: *Alan Yue*
Photos: *Stuart Lewis*
Circulation Manager: *Stanley Ezrol*

INTELLIGENCE DIRECTORS
Counterintelligence: *Jeffrey Steinberg, Michele Steinberg*
Economics: *John Hoefle, Marcia Merry Baker, Paul Gallagher*
History: *Anton Chaitkin*
Ibero-America: *Dennis Small*
Russia and Eastern Europe: *Rachel Douglas*
United States: *Debra Freeman*

INTERNATIONAL BUREAUS
Bogotá: *Miriam Redondo*
Berlin: *Rainer Apel*
Copenhagen: *Tom Gillesberg*
Houston: *Harley Schlanger*
Lima: *Sara Madueño*
Melbourne: *Robert Barwick*
Mexico City: *Gerardo Castilleja Chávez*
New Delhi: *Ramtanu Maitra*
Paris: *Christine Bierre*
Stockholm: *Ulf Sandmark*
United Nations, N.Y.C.: *Leni Rubinstein*
Washington, D.C.: *William Jones*
Wiesbaden: *Göran Haglund*

ON THE WEB
e-mail: eirns@larouchepub.com
www.larouchepub.com
www.executiveintelligencereview.com
www.larouchepub.com/eiw
Webmaster: *John Sigerson*
Assistant Webmaster: *George Hollis*
Editor, Arabic-language edition: *Hussein Askary*

EIR (ISSN 0273-6314) *is published weekly (50 issues), by EIR News Service, Inc., P.O. Box 17390, Washington, D.C. 20041-0390. (703) 777-9451*

European Headquarters: E.I.R. GmbH, Postfach Bahnstrasse 9a, D-65205, Wiesbaden, Germany
Tel: 49-611-73650
Homepage: http://www.eirna.com
e-mail: eirna@eirna.com
Director: Georg Neudecker

Montreal, Canada: 514-461-1557

Denmark: EIR - Danmark, Sankt Knuds Vej 11, basement left, DK-1903 Frederiksberg, Denmark. Tel.: +45 35 43 60 40, Fax: +45 35 43 87 57. e-mail: eirdk@hotmail.com.

Mexico City: EIR, Sor Juana Inés de la Cruz 242-2 Col. Agricultura C.P. 11360 Delegación M. Hidalgo, México D.F. Tel. (5525) 5318-2301 eirmexico@gmail.com

Canada Post Publication Sales Agreement #40683579

Postmaster: Send all address changes to *EIR*, P.O. Box 17390, Washington, D.C. 20041-0390.

Signed articles in *EIR* represent the views of the authors, and not necessarily those of the Editorial Board.

War Against Thermonuclear War

EIR Contents

www.larouchepub.com   Volume 42, Number 32, August 14, 2015

Cover This Week

Obama holds press conference at 2014 NATO summit in Wales.

White House Video

World on the Edge of the Nuclear Abyss: More Officials Get the Courage to Tell the Truth

by Helga Zepp-LaRouche

Aug. 7—Whereas it is no longer possible to ignore the signs that the U.S. Administration and NATO are preparing a military confrontation with Russia and China, perhaps even during this or next month, more and more leading personalities have found the courage, virtually at the last minute before the catastrophe, to break through the orchestrated charade (theater), which is aimed at using black propaganda to prepare the population for the coming war. The "Guns of August," the build-up toward the third, and, as Speaker of the Duma Sergei Naryshkin put it, humanity's *last* world war, is in full swing. But the way out is also within reach.

It is most remarkable that a former NATO Commander should express himself as follows. The Italian Lt. General Fabio Mini, formerly Chief of the General Staff for NATO's Southern Command and the Commander of KFOR in Kosovo, on the web-site "Critica Scientifica," issued a clear warning Aug. 6 that the current "world war" was escalating into a nuclear confrontation, and he linked this dynamic with the control of the financial markets over national states. He warned that today, limited wars are no longer possible, even theoretically, and that all the present conflicts—from the Cold War against Russia in the Baltic states, to Ukraine, to Syria and Yemen, including the so-called "low intensity conflicts"—in-

dicate that we must not expect a totally new conflict, but that we are already in it up to our necks.

"What is occurring in Asia with the Pacific strategic pivot," Lt. General Mini said, "is perhaps the clearest sign that the prospect of a World War II-like explosion is more probable in that theater. Not so much because aircraft carriers and missiles are being transferred there (which is indeed taking place), but because the preparation for a world war of that kind, including the inevitable

Russian State Duma

"If the logic of the Cold War is imposed on us, then we have to respond appropriately. And one should be very careful in using words such as 'redividing the world' or 'Third World War.' Both in our country and abroad. A Third World War would be mankind's last. And the strengthening of Russia's defense capabilities, including the funding decisions the Duma makes, is intended precisely to avert such a war."
　　　　　　—Sergey Naryshkin, in an interview with Izvestia July 30.

Here, Russian State Duma chairperson Naryshkin (right) speaks at a September 5, 2014 press conference in Moscow with OSCE official Iikka Kanerva.

nuclear confrontation, is what is being prepared. That is not to say that it will happen immediately, but the longer the preparation goes on, the more resources will go into weapons, and the more Asian and Western minds will orient to that direction." (see interview excerpts below)

On the occasion of the 70th anniversary of the dropping of atom bombs on Hiroshima and Nagasaki, an array of personalities has spoken out on the urgent necessity to ban and scrap nuclear weapons, due to their potential to wipe out humanity; interestingly, these include Japanese Prime Minister Shinzo

Department of Defense/Claudette Roulo

Army Lt. General Michael Flynn, then-head of the Defense Intelligence Agency, speaks at the Aspen Security Forum in Aspen, Colorado July 26, 2014.

Abe, but also the likely next leader of the British Labour Party, Jeremy Corbyn, as well as Mikhail Gorbachov. Gorbachov warned in an Aug. 6 interview with *Spiegel Online* that he was very worried about the danger of nuclear war, and that we might not survive the coming year if anyone in this overheated situation were to lose his nerve.

The American journalist Jack Hanick wrote in the *New York Observer* Aug. 4, under the headline "Can the U.S. Stop a War with Russia?," that the United States is preparing a war against Russia. But, [in defensive response,] Russia is also preparing for this war and will bring it to America, as the recent flights of the Bear-Bombers off the California coast on July 4 have shown. The American media of all political stripes have offered no critical analysis indicating that it would be necessary to take Russian arguments seriously, if serious consequences are to be avoided.

The United States is edging its way ever closer to a war against Russia; Democrats and Republicans are trying to outdo each other with provocative speeches, but history is full of examples of failed attempts to subdue Russia, Napoleon's and Hitler's being only the most recent examples.

Allying with Terrorists

The most spectacular interview, however, next to that of General Mini, has come from the former head of American Military Intelligence (DIA), Michael Flynn, on the "Head to Head" program on *Al-Jazeera* television Aug. 6. In that interview Flynn confirmed to inter-

viewer Mehdi Hasan, that he had not only studied a DIA Memorandum from 2012, according to which the West supported the creation of an Islamic state in Syria; but that the support by the White House for the radical jihadists—which then morphed into ISIL and al-Nusra—had been no error in judgment, but a conscious decision to play this card.

During the broadcast Hasan read the relevant sections of the 2012 memorandum, which had already been published pursuant to an FOIA court case. One section reads: "There is the possibility of establishing a declared or undeclared Salafist principality in Eastern Syria ... and this is exactly what the supporting powers to the opposition want, in order to isolate the Syrian regime...."

Hasan repeatedly asked during the interview, whether the U.S. Administration had turned a blind eye in respect to the report, in response to which Flynn repeatedly emphasized that this had been a conscious decision. Earlier releases from this DIA report suggested that the U.S. Administration had organized the arming of al-Qaeda, al-Nusra, the Muslim Brotherhood, and ISIS, in full knowledge that these groups intended to set up a Caliphate in eastern Syria and Iraq, in order to overthrow the Assad regime. Flynn underscored that the DIA had not only produced this memorandum in 2012, but that he had repeatedly spoken with the White House and the National Security Council and warned of the consequences which would occur if these organizations were armed.

This interview was extraordinarily explosive, because three days after the U.S. Congress left on July 29 for its summer recess, President Obama—naturally without the consent of the Congress that the Constitution prescribes—changed the rules of engagement for the U.S. Airforce in Syria, so that it would, from now on, be permitted to defend the American-trained Syrian rebels (55 men!), including against the Syrian Air Force. That is, to all intents and purposes, an open pathway to military strikes against Syria.

Exactly such a decision had been prevented in September 2013, literally at the last moment, when the

Chairman of the Joint Chiefs of Staff (JCS), Gen. Martin Dempsey, very well briefed by Flynn, spoke with Obama shortly before the already-ordered military operation against Syria, and warned him, that it would lead to impeachment proceedings, if he did not obtain Congress's permission for this war. Obama saw that he was forced to consult Congress, and, sensing that he would lose the vote, the President ultimately pulled back from a decision that would have had unforeseen consequences.

One Minute to Midnight

For Flynn, in the current situation, to bring into the open the truth about the background of the evolution of the ISIS terrorists, is obviously of the highest strategic importance. Because today, as two years ago, the attempt to eradicate the Assad government with the help of Islamic terrorists, threatens to provoke a confrontation in the whole region, and beyond. After Obama's announcement, Russian Foreign Minister Sergei Lavrov immediately warned that military strikes against the Syrian army would complicate the war against ISIS, and remarked ironically, that most of the "moderate" rebels trained by the U.S. end up within a very short time in the ranks of the terrorists.

Russia's President Vladimir Putin at the same time gave Turkish President Recep Tayyip Erdogan a sharp warning, that his bombing of the Kurds in Syria endangered the war against ISIS. Russia maintains the Tartus base in Syria, which, in the event of the overthrow of Assad, would fall into the hands of ISIS.

It is literally one minute to midnight, to carry out an open debate on the failed policy in Southwest Asia, if an escalation into the worst-scenario catastrophe is to be stopped. Because the trail of destruction leads from Iraq—against which a war based on lies was started wantonly—to Afghanistan, then Libya, Syria, and Yemen.

Jeremy Corbyn, the probable new head of the British Labour Party, has just demanded that Tony Blair be held accountable for war crimes, if the Chilcot Report proves his guilt in the realization of the war against Iraq. What is proven in any case is the complete failure of the policy of regime change, with the help of terrorists, in this region; terrorists who will then be bombed in order to create new terrorists.

In October, NATO will hold a series of maneuvers

The Syrian "moderate opposition" photographed in October 2012. "We told our U.S. colleagues that the most important [thing] is, that up until now, all examples of U.S. instructors training militants, the so-called moderate opposition, on the territory of neighboring countries, resulted in the vast majority of those militants ending up on the extremists' side."— Russian Foreign Minister Sergey Lavrov, at a Qatar press conference August 3.

among which is one with the name Trident Juncture 15, the largest one of its kind in 25 years. In that maneuver, among other things, a deployment of nuclear weapons against Russia will be simulated. In the same time frame, JCS Chairman Dempsey and a range of other high-ranking military leaders will be replaced by successors, several among whom have already declared that Russia is Enemy No. 1 for the United States.

Mankind has never found itself so close to the edge of its potential extinction. It is of vital importance that Germany and all the other European nations make perfectly clear that they are having no part of a possible war against Russia and China.

There are a whole slew of measures which could be taken. Among them are the immediate ending of sanctions against Russia; the immediate ban and destruction of nuclear weapons—beginning with those stationed in Europe—and an honest discussion about the failed policy in southwest Asia in reference to the DIA memo. Likewise, it is urgent to put on the table the solution to the strategic challenges now threatening all mankind, challenges such as terrorism, the refugee catastrophe, drugs, famine, and so forth,—for whose solution cooperation with Russia and China is decisive. We urgently need citizens who will no longer allow mediocre governments, led by Great Britain and the United States, to sleepwalk into World War III.

Sputnik Interviews Helga Zepp-LaRouche

Aug. 7—Following a radio interview with Helga Zepp-LaRouche today, Russia's Sputnik News published the following news release, under the title "U.S. Analyst Claims Geopolitics Could Lead to Extinction of Human Race." The article included a link to a 7-minute excerpt of the interview, which is transcribed below. The mp3 audio file is available here.

Lyndon LaRouche's wife, Helga Zepp-LaRouche spoke to Sputnik about how U.S. atomic bombing in Nagasaki and Hiroshima was completely unnecessary and how the United States is preparing for another atomic war against Russia and China right now.

For 70 years, the destruction of Hiroshima and Nagasaki by the United States has been marked by reverence for the many victims who tragically lost their lives during the nuclear attack, but now an influential American international affairs outlet, *Foreign Policy*, has decided to spin the event, blaming the Soviet Union for what happened.

In his article "Did Hiroshima Save Japan From Soviet Occupation?" Sergey Radchenko makes it seem like the nuclear bombings were a godsend, and that the United States humanely intended to save Japan from communism.

Following the publication of the provocative article, Helga Zepp-LaRouche, founder of the international Schiller Institutes, spoke to Sputnik radio, saying that there is no justification for what the United States did in Japan.

There was absolutely no reason for this bombing as there was already peace negotiation between the emperor and the Vatican at that time. The bombing was done to instigate horror and awe by Truman so that he could continue the era of imperialism.

"There are many people who have been warning that the U.S. and NATO are preparing a new war against Russia and China. There is a very serious escalation of the situation, making the month of August extremely dangerous as history shows most of the wars started in August, and the U.S. military has changed tactic in Syria last week and the U.S. Congress has gone into recess.

She goes on to say that the United States is busily preparing itself for war. Signs indicate that another nuclear war is getting closer and this time it will annihilate the entire human race.

In order to prevent that from happening, LaRouche said that the United States, Russia and China need to sit down and talk. Europe must apply pressure, and say that it will not be a part of such a war.

"The leaders of the U.S., Russia and China must sit together and discuss the new international security architecture. We must overcome geopolitics if we don't want to extinct ourselves." Below is the transcript of the interview.

Transcript

Helga Zepp-LaRouche: I think historically it is now well-established that there was absolutely no reason for this bombing, because there were already peace negotiations between the Emperor and the Vatican at that time. And therefore the argument that it was to save American soldiers, is completely fraudulent. I think the bombing occurred to establish an aura of *Schrecklichkeit,* of horror, of awe, to basically—this was Truman, and it was a way to start to establish a post-war order in order to continue the rule of colonialism and imperialism, which would not have happened if Franklin D. Roosevelt would have been alive.

Sputnik: And let's look at these poll findings, from the Japanese. The majority of Japanese don't share the point of view presented by foreign policy, so the question here, Helga, is, who and why is someone trying to rewrite history?

Zepp-LaRouche: Yes, but I think it is part of the present logic. I think there are many people in the last period who have been warning that the United States and NATO are preparing a new war, this time against Russia and China. Even the *Observer* has an article to this effect. My husband, Mr. Lyndon LaRouche, has warned at the end of June already, that the most dangerous period would be the month of August. First of all, because all world wars in the past century have started in August, and he said the most dangerous period is when the U.S. Congress goes into recess. And unfortunately, this was totally confirmed, because the U.S. Congress went into recess last Wednesday, a week ago, and on Friday, the U.S. changed the rules of engagement for the U.S. Air Force in Syria, and that was done without announcement, without approval of Congress, and it was only then leaked the following Sunday by the Wall Street Journal.

Now this means a very serious escalation, because it brings the world back to exactly the situation where it was two years ago, when the U.S. Congress voted against military strikes against Syria. So this time, the Congress is out of session, and this was changed—this is unfortunately only one aspect. You have to look at the totality of the situation.

You have the modernization of tactical nuclear weapons in Europe, the B61 and B61-12, which could indicate an attack being brought into the Russian territory by F-35 stealth bombers, and there are many people who are extremely concerned that this is a preparation for a regional nuclear theatre in Europe. You have to add to that the fact that the United States did *not* stop the U.S. missile defense system in Eastern Europe after the Iran P5+1 agreement was successfully concluded, and that confirms what Russia has said many times: that this U.S. missile defense system was never meant for missiles from Iran, but it was always directed against Russia.

And then, at the recent and present ASEAN forum

Unsurvivable

A dark, gruesome, but wholly true depiction of the threat of thermonuclear war, its consequences, and Obama's deployment of a major portion of the U.S. thermonuclear capabilities in multiple theaters threatening both Russia and China.

http://larouchepac.com/unsurvivable

in Malaysia, Foreign Minister Lavrov just warned correctly, that there is a huge military buildup in the Pacific. Obviously, what is the purpose of these aircraft carriers and other systems being brought there?

So I think the signs are overwhelming that there *is* a war preparation, and I think there will be a maneuver in September which basically will be—it's called the Trident Juncture 15— which will rehearse the use of nuclear weapons against Russia.

All of these signs are overwhelmingly worrisome, and I think we need, really, a complete mobilization of the world public, because this *is* the eve of World War III, and it has to be stopped. Because if it happens, I don't think it will be a regional theatre; I think it will, by the nature of thermonuclear weapons, it will be a global thermonuclear war, in which case there will be probably nobody left alive. So, we are really looking at the annihilation of mankind, and that is where we are at.

Sputnik: At this point, Helga, what should be done? Who should sit down and talk?

Zepp-LaRouche: Well, I think there must be made an absolute effort that the United States, Russia, and China are sitting together at one table, and all the other leaders of the world who are concerned, should make maximum pressure that this occurs. Europe could do a big role, if Europe would say, we are not part of such a war, and we insist that the United States and Russia and China, the leaders, sit together, and discuss the new international security architecture.

I think President Xi Jinping has given a very good example when he offered to President Obama at the recent APEC meeting last year, in Beijing, the win-win policy of cooperation with the New Silk Road. He has said that we have to have a world order in which cooperation among major nations occurs for the common benefit of everybody, a win-win strategy.

And I think, that if we have learned anything from the geopolitical wars in the Twentieth Century, then the lesson must be that, if we don't want to make ourselves extinct, we must overcome geopolitics. Geopolitics is what causes world wars. And that we must move to a new paradigm in the history of civilization, a new era, which is defined by the common aims of mankind as one humanity first, and then you can settle regional questions after you have agreed on these common aims of mankind.

And that is the all-demanding question of this moment.

'Inevitable Nuclear Confrontation, Is What Is Being Prepared'

Aug. 7—Lt. Gen. Fabio Mini, former chief of Staff of the NATO Southern Command and former commander of KFOR in Kosovo, has warned of an escalation of the current ongoing "world war" into a nuclear confrontation, and has connected this dynamic to the power of financial markets over nation-states.

Mini issued those statements in an Aug. 6 interview with Italian biologist Enzo Pennetta on his website "Critica Scientifica." Pennetta has authorized EIR to reproduce major excerpts of the interview.

General Mini's views are not necessarily those of EIR, but we find some of them unusually sagacious.

NATO

Lieutenant General Fabio Mini, former chief of Staff of the NATO Southern Command and former commander of KFOR in Kosovo.

Q: General, in your book *La Guerra spiegata a... (War Explained...)*,[1] you state that there are no limited wars, or better, that a power engaging in a limited war, in reality is preparing a total war. In the current situation of spreading conflict, which seems to follow a sort of fault line going from Ukraine to Yemen, through Syria and Iraq, should we then expect the breakout of a total conflict?

Mini: The category of limited wars, discussed by Clausewitz himself, was meant to include conflicts with limited objectives and thus, limited instruments and resources to be employed. War should be the minimal [effort] for achieving political aims. War was a continuation of politics. However, the risks that the conflict could

degenerate and enlarge, both in response to the enemy's reaction and to the appetites for war—which increase by eating—were evident. With a careful management of alliances and neutralities, a conflict could be limited in operation, and still have a broader political significance.

Today, a limited war is no longer possible, not even in theory; the political and economic interests involved in each conflict, including the most remote and insignificant one, involve all major powers as well as everyone's pockets and consciences. War has become a violation of international law and is no longer the continuation of politics, but its denial, its failure. Despite that (or maybe even because of that), the aim of a war is not enough to justify it, and those who start a war demonstrate political incompetence and assume responsibility for a conflict whose aims and outcome they do not know.

With the introduction of global control of conflicts and global management of security (including through the United Nations), all states and all rulers are responsible for conflicts. And all conflicts are global, if not under the aspect of military intervention, definitely in their economic, social, and moral consequences.

Thus, starting with the Cold War launched by the Baltic countries against Russia, to the American 'covert' war against Russia itself, to the Russian claims against Ukraine, to Syria, to Yemen, and all other so-called minor or "low-intensity" conflicts, everything indicates that we don't have to wait for another total conflict: We are already up to our neck in it.

What is occurring in Asia with the Pacific strategic

---

1. Fabio Mini, *La Guerra spiegata a...*, Einaudi, Turin, January 2013.

pivot is perhaps the clearest sign that the prospect of a World War II-like explosion is more probable in that theater. Not so much because aircraft carriers and missiles are being transferred there (which is indeed taking place), but because the preparation for a world war of that kind, including the inevitable nuclear confrontation, is what is being prepared. That is not to say that it will happen immediately, but the longer the preparation goes on, the more resources will go into weapons, and the more Asian and Western minds will orient to that direction. ...

Q: Another interesting reflection of yours, concerns the fact that war always leads to a different policy than the one that preceded and prepared the war. Should we therefore be prepared for a different world from the one which is generating current conflicts? And if yes, do you have an idea in which direction we are moving?

Mini: I would say yes, but I do not think we can have many illusions about the outcome. We are living in a very important period of historical transition: the global system established by the winners of WWII is cracking; blocs have disappeared; many political regimes created by colonial powers are in a crisis; Africa wakes up one day and regresses the next day; economic issues overwhelm political, social, and military issues; the peripheries of big powers and their satraps are seeking indifferently either greater autonomy or stricter serfdom. Current conflicts are the most evident signs of this process, which will lead to a new formulation of international relationships and balances.

However, it is not self-evident that this transition will lead to a so-called "new world order." Pushes for change and stability are still weak, and risk-making conflicts and post-conflict situations chronic; the latter are as dangerous as conflicts. There are signs of strong resistance to change in a multipolar sense by some rich as well as some poor countries. The richer countries are again orienting towards a power-policy, especially through military means; the poorer countries are orienting towards resignation to slavery.

The so-called "new order" might be the old order of the colonial model, and armed forces are orienting more and more towards the system of "police armies" (constabulary forces). In many African countries there is nostalgia for the colonial period, or colonial countries are accused of abandoning them. Power and slavery are

complementary. A Chinese philosopher said about his people: "There have been centuries when the desire to be a slave has been satisfied, and others when it was not. ..."

Q: In your book, you explain how war has evolved through the centuries. Now a fifth-generation war, or limitless war, has been theorized, i.e. a war that must not be perceived as such, and which includes financial means. Can we say that we are in the middle of such a war?

Mini: No question about it. But even this fifth-generation war is transforming itself into the sixth-genera-

> This fifth-generation war is transforming itself into the sixth-generation war: gang war. The aims of such wars are not merely security, and nations are no longer the sole players; we are in the hands of "gangs" with their own aims and without any scruples except for their own prosperity at the expense of others.

tion war: gang war. The aims of such wars are not merely security, and nations are no longer the sole players; we are in the hands of "gangs" with their own aims and without any scruples except for their own prosperity at the expense of others. Gangs move without the constraints of borders and means, without respect, only pursuing profit. They tend to elude international law and legality, they tend to bend states themselves to their interests, and to control states' policies and weapons. Today, the concern of armies and police apparatuses is not to understand why they work, but for whom. If the state, by definition, must (or should) care for the common good, the gang cares only for the private, non-state, and often anti-state, good.

In 2004, I asked an American colonel what war he was fighting in Iraq, and he replied, "This is a gang war, and we are the biggest gang." He too, had understood that he was not working for a nation or for the common good, but for something that went beyond his role of defending the public: he was a mercenary, like many others, serving someone who paid. For that reason, he considered himself to be a war "professional."

Finance is the only really global and instantaneous system and it uses both legal and illegal means: exactly like any modern gang of criminals. The command structure of gangs has two reference models: the paternalist-vertical model and the committee-horizontal model. The latter is prevailing over the former even if, at certain hierarchical levels, there is always someone stronger than the others. The horizontal model is also the one that best succeeds in covering internal and external wars. There are contingent interests that often bring adversaries onto the same side.

Q: The concept of war as "instrument of domination" also emerges from your book, i.e., an instrument to force a certain party to act against its own will. In the recent case of Greece, in which the popular will had to concede to contrary requests from Europe, can we call this an act of war?

Mini: In this case too, we must refer to limitless war and, unfortunately, to gang war. Greece has suffered from a diktat which, by bending the will of the government and of the population itself, is certainly an act of war. However, the real scandal with Greece is not in the diktat imposed, but in the apparent laxness on the side of the very international institutions which should have overseen its financial state.

The financial war against Greece is almost a perfect gang war. Only some fool could really think that Greece doctored its figures without the knowledge of the EU, the ECB, the IMF, the Federal Reserve, the World Bank, or the prosperous and omniscient rating agencies. It is much more realistic to think that, at the moment of the changeover to the euro, political interests in Europe prevailed over the financial,[2] and that it was the financial interests that loaded the most fragile members with the maximum possible debt.

We have a short memory, but well before 2001, the debate on the euro assumed that many countries on the European periphery and next in line to become members (northern and eastern Europe), could not possibly comply with the parameters imposed. It is no accident that only the countries on the periphery were the first induced to go into debt and then into default, or to be "saved" from the frying pan by going into the fire. Ireland, Great Britain, Portugal, Spain, Italy, and Greece have been the most evident examples of a maneuver which was neither carried out nor favored by nations, but run by institutions which call themselves supranational, and are in any case modeled on the private interests of the so-called "market" system.

---

2. In other words, the political decision to eliminate national sovereignty took precedence over financial common sense. As no lesser an authority than former French Presidential adviser Jacques Attali admitted years later, it was known from the beginning that the imposition of the euro would lead to national crises, but this was seen as a necessary step toward forcing total political integration/consolidation in Europe.

The British Empire Roots of American Social Control

by Barbara Boyd

Introduction: The Case of Donald Trump

August 10—Here we are, already far into the war declared by Wall Street and the City of London against Russia and China, with President Obama marching us step-by-step to early nuclear conflagration. The population which should be on its feet, demanding survival, not just for itself but for the entire human race, by insisting on Obama's impeachment, is, instead, distracted—restive, agitated, knowing something is deeply wrong, but distracted. The heirs of the great Washington, Hamilton, John Quincy Adams, Lincoln, and Franklin Roosevelt must create and shape a new great Presidency right now if they are to survive, let alone experience their own actual humanity.

The national debate, however, does not concern the imminence of war and how to prevent it; rather, we are enticed to be preoccupied with the likes of Donald Trump. We are bombarded with police shootings, chaos, the disintegration of our immediate environment. This is not accidental.

By focusing on the methods and history of those who create this controlled and manufactured environment,—namely, the national security *gendarmerie* in the Federal Bureau of Investigation (FBI) and related agencies, and their public opinion propagandists,—we could find the keys to defeating the British Empire itself.

This is a short introduction, to what will be a longer article in the *EIR* next week, about the historical methods of popular subversion used by the FBI against the American population.

Roy M. Cohn in 1964

cc/Michael Vadon

Donald Trump at the 2015 Conservative Political Action Conference.

The Satanic Roy Cohn

We begin with the case of Donald Trump. He is, as Lyndon LaRouche points out, a product of J. Edgar Hoover's New York circles, a coterie which included mobbed-up businessmen like Lewis Rosenstiel, along with Cardinal Spellman of the New York archdiocese, and various Wall Street establishment and media figures, all presided over by Hoover's main New York man, the satanic Roy M. Cohn. Cohn was Trump's lawyer and best friend throughout most of Trump's formative years—his mentor, according to Trump.

Those who know their history, know that Roy Cohn was the legal assassin deployed by J. Edgar Hoover and Joseph McCarthy during the notorious manufactured "Red Scare" of the 1950s, which destroyed the lives of numerous innocent public servants and others, while instilling fear and cowardice in the post-war U.S. population.

When McCarthy was finally discredited in the Army-McCarthy hearings or 1954, Cohn left Washington for New York City, where he became the favorite lawyer and facilitator for New York-New Jersey organized crime, defrauding his clients, bribing judges, and corrupting and blackmailing much of what was New York celebrity, journalistic, and high-society culture in the 1960s through the 1980s. Cohn threw exclusive sex and drug parties at Studio 54, Le Club, and other "hot" night spots. Trump claims that he and Cohn met at Le Club.

At the same time, Cohn was the lawyer and a personal confidant of New York's Cardinal Spellman, himself an FBI informant and J. Edgar Hoover crony. Roy Cohn did all of this while being protected by Hoover's FBI and other Wall Street-controlled secret government entities, who gladly accepted the dirt he provided them about those he seduced, in return for allowing his gross and satanic criminality. He was only disbarred on his deathbed, as he was dying of AIDS.

Organized Crime

Donald Trump's early fortune was inherited from his father Fred, who was a developer of military housing during the war years, and middle-class housing in Queens and Brooklyn after World War II. Like his son, Fred had numerous dealings with New York's organized crime families, according to accounts by Wayne Barrett, who has written extensively about the Trumps.

Donald Trump's mentor, Roy Cohn, represented Anthony "Fat Tony" Salerno, the boss of the Genovese organized crime family, and, it is alleged, Trump met with Salerno at Cohn's Manhattan offices. Salerno's company, S&A Concrete, was used by Trump in constructing several of his New York City buildings. According to numerous published reports, Trump's initial project in Atlantic City, the casino which became Trump Plaza, was built on land which Trump bought at twice its market value from Salvatore Testa, a made man in the Philadelphia mafia and son of Philip "Chicken Man" Testa, who briefly headed the Philly mob after Angelo Bruno's 1980 killing. The casino was built in part by construction companies owned by the Philly mob.

Trump also had a close association with Kenneth Shapiro, a banker for the Nicky Scarfo who became head of the Philly mob after Philip Testa was blown up. Recently, Trump has worked to distance himself from Felix Sater, a fraudster with mafia ties who worked with Trump on numerous occasions. Sater's ties to American and Russian mobsters have been widely reported, as well as his work as a government provocateur and informant.

Trump's campaign manager, until his recent "resignation," was Roger Stone, described by Trump as a long-time close friend and associate. Stone is a long-standing Republican Party dirty-tricks operative who cut his teeth with Richard Nixon's CREEP. According to Stone, he has Richard Nixon's picture tattooed on his back.

Nixon's entire career, of course, was closely associated with, and protected by, J. Edgar Hoover and the FBI. Stone's most recent publicized antics, other than involvement in his own sex scandal, involved his work for the Bush family in securing George W. Bush's presidency, by orchestrating a riot which stopped the 2000 Florida vote recount. He also played a central role in the sex scandal which ended the political career of Eliot Spitzer, who was reviled and set up because he had devoted his public career to taking down Wall Street.

Deadly Silence

Everything I have written here about Trump is readily and publicly available. Yet, millions of Americans say they are seriously considering this man for the presidency; all the so-called Republican candidates are silent about this perverse story,—a silence which itself should disqualify them all from the Presidency. And again, this reality-TV escapade proceeds while in actual reality, Barack Obama takes step after step on the path to war.

Next week, we will document the British Empire origins and Twentieth Century backdrop to this operation.

Ulysses S. Grant's Moral Crusade for Peace—1865-1879

by Robert Ingraham

This article includes contributions from Dennis Speed, William Jones, and Frank Scaturro.

> *"Let us have peace"*
> —Motto at Grant's Tomb,
> Riverside Park, Manhattan

On March 3, 1864 President Abraham Lincoln promoted Ulysses S. Grant to Lieutenant General, giving him command of all Union Armies. Two months later, General Grant led his Army across the Rapidan River in Virginia, initiating the Overland Campaign. Between May 4th and June 12th, the troops under Grant's command fought fourteen battles with the Army of Northern Virginia. There were over 100,000 casualties in fewer than fifty days. By the end of the campaign, Robert E. Lee's army was shattered as Lee retreated into a defensive siege at Petersburg, leading to his eventual surrender at Appomattox Court House in April of 1865.

Only days after Lee's surrender, on Good Friday, President Abraham Lincoln was assassinated in Washington D.C. Thus began the test of National Leadership that fate thrust upon Ulysses S. Grant, for, during the next fourteen years, it would be Grant who would assume the mantle of

wikimedia.org

First as Commanding General of the United States Army, then as President of the United States, for twelve years Ulysses S. Grant personally led the fight for full equality and opportunity for all Americans, the Constitutional notion of an American Citizen, against the ongoing war by the Confederacy.

Lincoln, and who would provide the quality of Presidential leadership which saved the American Republic and re-established the nation's commitment to the principles enshrined in the Constitution of the United States.

First as Commanding General of the United States Army, then as President of the United States, for twelve years Ulysses Grant personally led the fight for full citizenship for black Americans. This commitment to full equality and opportunity for all Americans, i.e., to the notion of an *"American Citizen"* as such was created at the Constitutional Convention by George Washington, Alexander Hamilton, and Gouverneur Morris, extended to Grant's approach to dealing with the American Indians during his Presidency, as well as to his fight for free national public education for all Americans, regardless of wealth, race or religion.

Both during his two terms as President and later during his two-and-one-half year long World Tour, Grant challenged the world to emulate the Constitutional System of America. Between 1877 and 1879, in meetings with numerous world leaders, Grant intervened forcefully against the policies and "principles" of the British Empire, counterposing the American example as the means by which peace and cooperation among nations might be secured. In many of those discussions, Grant made clear that it was not just the military might, nor the economic power of the United States that other nations should admire. Rather, he repeatedly pointed to his nation's battle to end slavery and the efforts to secure successful Reconstruction of the South, which represented the key philosophical approach to transforming the world away from the tradition of Empire.

Grant's anti-imperial Crusade for Peace holds many lessons for us today. It points the way towards a New World, a vision which we see glimmers of in the magnificent recent completion of the Second Suez Canal by the nation of Egypt and the New Silk Road perspective of the Shanghai Cooperation Organization and the Chinese government. All men *are* brothers, and all share in the divine creative nature of our species. That is the eternal message which comes down to us from the American struggle of 1861 through 1879, and we would be wise to heed it.

I. Commander of the Armies— 1865-1869

Treat the Negro as a citizen and as a voter, as he is and must remain, and soon parties will be divided, not on the color line, but on principle. Then we shall have no complaint of sectional interference.

Ulysses Grant

The Thirteenth Amendment to the United States Constitution, abolishing slavery and involuntary servitude, was passed by the U.S. Senate on April 8, 1864 and by the House of Representatives on January 31, 1865. Anticipating early ratification of the Amendment, in March of 1865, at the request of President Abraham Lincoln, Congress established the Freedmen's Bureau, under the jurisdiction of the Department of War and led by Union Army General Oliver Howard.

The Freedmen's Bureau was charged with overseeing the process of emancipation in the Southern States and securing the rights of "life, liberty and the pursuit of happiness" for the new black citizens of America. During its tumultuous existence, the primary historic contribution made by the Freedmen's Bureau was its creation of an extensive network of both primary and university schools for freed blacks throughout the South.

Prior to the Civil War, no southern state had a system of universal public education, and all the states prohibited slaves from gaining an education. The Bureau spent $5 million to set up schools for blacks. As early as late-1865, more than 90,000 former slaves were enrolled as students in public schools. By 1870, there were more than 1,000 schools for freedmen in the South, and such was this sustained effort, that by 1877, 571,000 black children were in school. At the same time, between 1866 and 1872, an estimated twenty-five institutions of higher learning for black youth were established. These included the Richmond Union (1865), Fisk University (1866), and Howard University 1867).

By late 1865, President Andrew Johnson had revealed himself as a bitter opponent of both black equality and the post-war vision of Abraham Lincoln. Johnson's intention was to block all efforts at black suffrage in the South, return the Southern blacks to a status of *de facto*, if not *de jure*, slavery, and to re-establish the full voting strength of the Confederate States, in alliance with the Copperheads of the North, to take back control of the nation from the Republican Party. In 1865 and 1866, state after state in the South, with the approval of President Johnson, enacted *Black Codes* that eliminated all civil rights for blacks in the South and created legal and economic conditions almost indistinguishable from slavery.

In November 1865, Johnson sent General Grant on a fact-finding mission to the South. The conditions which Grant found during this trip convinced him of two things: that full equality for the former slaves was the only basis for peace in the nation, and that the only institution capable of enforcing the needed transformation in the South was the United States Army, of which he was the Commanding General. Almost simultaneous to Grant's trip, in December 1865, the Ku Klux Klan was founded by a group of Confederate veterans in Pulaski, Tennessee, and the war which ensued between the Union Army and a Klan made up almost entirely of Confederate veterans, was nothing less than a continuation of the Civil War under new conditions.

On May 1st, 1866 a "riot" erupted in Memphis, Tennessee. Over three days forty-six blacks were murdered, but the violence was not indiscriminate; it focused especially on the homes (and wives) of black Union soldiers. Less than three months later a well-planned attack, misnamed a riot, took place in New Orleans in which 238 former slaves, who had been peacefully marching for civil rights, were killed by well-armed groups of whites. Federal troops stopped the massacre, jailing many of the white attackers, mostly former Confederate soldiers. Louisiana military commander Philip Sheridan later stated, "It was no riot; it was an absolute massacre . . . a murder which the mayor and the police of the city perpetrated without the shadow of a necessity."

In the 1866 Congressional elections, the Southern States, largely still under the control of white former Confederates, elected to the United States Congress a combined delegation which included the vice-president of the Confederacy (Alexander Stephens), four Confederate Generals, five Confederate colonels, six Confederate cabinet members, and fifty-eight Confederate Congressmen. None of them ever took their seats. Despite President Johnson's view that all of these un-repentant secessionists should be seated in Congress, almost all were either prevented from leaving their home states by Union troops, or were arrested on the way to Washington, D.C., by order of General Ulysses Grant.

In response to these developments, during 1866, Congress enacted a series of laws, including the Civil Rights Act of 1866 and the Fourteenth Amendment to the U.S. Constitution. In 1867, Congress passed the Military Reconstruction Act, the Second Military Reconstruction Act and the Third Military Reconstruction Act. These acts divided the South into five military districts, placing the entirety of the former Confederacy under U.S. military occupation. No state was allowed to form a government, nor to elect representatives to Congress, until they called new constitutional conventions, provided for black suffrage, and ratified the Fourteenth Amendment.

The five U.S. military commanders in the South were instructed to register eligible voters, establish a timetable for holding constitutional conventions, and set up machinery for ratification. Local mayors, sher-

The Mission: President Lincoln and his military commanders depicted in George P.A. Healy's 1868 painting, "The Peacemakers," during their consultation on the terms of the South's surrender on the steamer River Queen a few days before Appomattox. From left to right: General William T. Sherman, General Ulysses S. Grant, President Abraham Lincoln, and Admiral David Porter.

iffs, and other civilian officials who refused to go along with the military orders were either removed from office or jailed by Union commanders.

Under the Third Military Reconstruction Act, the Southern state governments were made subordinate to the military district commanders—who were given explicit authority to remove civil officials and appoint replacements. Voter registration boards were authorized to reject potential voters believed to have perjured themselves concerning their prior allegiance. General Grant was granted full authority to ensure that the Reconstruction Acts were faithfully enforced.

In New Orleans, General Sheridan ordered the desegregation of streetcars and the admission of blacks to jury duty. On March 27th he discharged the Mayor of New Orleans, the state attorney general, and a district judge. Later he removed the white supremacist governor.[1] Grant wired his immediate support, "It is just the thing. I approve what you have done. I have no doubt it will also meet with the approval from the reconstructed."

----

1. Earlier, with Grant's approval, Sheridan had deposed the governor of Texas, holding him responsible for the upsurge of violence in the state.

In the Carolinas, General Daniel Sickles issued orders revising the civil and criminal codes to remove discriminatory provisions that denied the freedmen equal justice. General John Schofield, commanding in Virginia, offered military protection "in cases where the civil authorities fail to give such protection."

Congress enacted the Reconstruction Acts, but it was to Grant, and Grant alone, that the full weight of the enforcement of the Acts was given, and he attacked the obstacles with the same tenacity and sense of mission he had demonstrated during the War.

Between November 1867 and January 1868, state constitutional conventions were held in Alabama, Louisiana, Georgia, Virginia, Mississippi, Arkansas, South Carolina, Florida, and North Carolina. These assemblies adopted revolutionary constitutions. The full racial integration of public accommodations, generalized public education for white and black males, as well as, in some cases women, and redistribution of land were implemented. The right of women to vote nearly passed the South Carolina Legislature. South Carolina went from having 500 teachers and approximately 5000 public school pupils, to 3000 teachers, 1000 of them black, responsible for 30,000 pupils, in approximately eight years.

As early as 1865 Union military commanders had first appointed black men to political posts in the post-insurrection South. Once African-Americans received the right to vote in 1867, they used it vigorously. Two-thirds of the new South Carolina legislature were Blacks. In descending order, the states of Mississippi, Louisiana, Florida, Alabama, Arkansas, Texas, Georgia, North Carolina, and Virginia had significant,if not majority, African-American representatives. Even in the nearly-purely-evil state of Mississippi, black people won fifty-five out of one hundred fifteen House seats and nine out of thirty-seven seats in the State Senate. On the state level in 1873, black men served as secretary of state, superintendent of education, commissioner of immigration, commissioner of agriculture, and lieutenant governor. Two African-American Senators and fifteen Representatives were elected to the United States Congress.

All of these accomplishments were achieved under essentially war-time conditions. By 1868 the Ku Klux Klan had about a half million members, mostly Confederate veterans who deployed as military units without uniform. This was nothing less than irregular warfare against the Federal Republic. Opposed to them were

Library of Congress

An 1867 drawing depicting African-Americans exercising their right to vote.

white and black federal troops and militia, as well as governors, state legislators, and others who were determined to implement the Union perspective.

In Washington, D.C., Johnson began removing the Grant-allied Commanders of the Southern Military Districts. Sheridan was the first to be fired, followed by the Commanders in the districts of Georgia-Alabama-Florida and in Mississippi-Arkansas. In response, Grant, acting under the authority vested in him by the Third Reconstruction Act, issued Special Orders No. 429 forbidding the new district commanders from restoring civilian officials deposed by their predecessors. The following day his staff released to the press Grant's letter to Johnson protesting Sheridan's removal. When Sheridan's replacement, Gen. Winfield Scott Hancock, assumed command in New Orleans, he initially issued orders nullifying many of Sheridan's policies and declaring the state's civil authority paramount. Grant immediately reversed all of Hancock's orders. President Johnson responded by sending a special message to Congress censuring Grant.

From 1865 to 1869, as Commanding General of the United States Army, it was Ulysses Grant who directed the battle for human freedom in the South. He never wavered in this mission, nor in his commitment to continue Abraham Lincoln's revolution. Emancipation was enforced by Union troops. Black schools and Universities were protected by regiments of Union Soldiers.[2] Secessionists and Confederate loyalists were removed from office, and between 1867 and 1877 truly democratic elections were held throughout the South, including the 1872 election which has been called the most democratic election in U.S. history until 1968.[3] As Grant stated on several occasions, these actions were the pre-condition for the true unification of the nation, under the Constitution, overcoming all sectional interests. All of this was carried out under Grant's direction and at his command.

Executive Treason

In 1866, General Grant received reports that President Johnson might be planning a *coup d'état* to prevent a Republican victory in November. Johnson had already asked Attorney General Henry Stanbery for an opinion as to the legitimacy of the 39th Congress. Rumors swirled that the President contemplated recognizing a new Congress made up of Southern representatives and cooperative Northern Democrats. When asked for his view on such an action, Grant replied, "The army will support the Congress as it now is and disperse the other."

To prevent the possibility of an Administration-supported Southern insurrection, Grant quietly ordered the removal of weapons and ammunition from federal arsenals in the South. He then wrote Sheridan warning him to be on guard. "I much fear that we are fast approaching the point where he will want to declare [Congress] itself illegal, unconstitutional and revolutionary. Commanders in the Southern states will have to take great care to see, if a crisis does come, that no armed headway can be made against the Union." By mid-October Grant canceled plans to attend the wedding of his aide Colonel Orville Babcock. "I cannot fully explain to you the reason," he wrote Congressman Elihu Washburne, "but it will

___

2. In fact, many of the new black Southern Universities were established on the grounds of then-existing Union troop encampments, under direct military protection.

3. It should be stated that the true democratic nature of these elections is measured not simply in the number of black voters, but also in the millions of poor white Southerners who were also enfranchised for the first time in history.

not do for me to leave Washington before the elections."

Grant's fear of a presidential coup was not unfounded. With two weeks remaining before the election, Johnson was pressing to deploy federal troops in Maryland to support the white supremacist state government against the Union Army in Baltimore. The issue involved adding ex-rebels to the voting lists, many of whom did not qualify. City registrars were opposed to adding the names, and the governor was threatening to replace the officials with men more sympathetic. Wearing civilian clothes, Grant visited the city twice in the next ten days to mediate the dispute. In the end, the election came and went peacefully.

The Democrats claimed victory, Johnson rejoiced, but the Democratic victory in Maryland was the exception in 1866. Elsewhere Johnson's supporters were swept away in a Republican landslide. The election turned into a referendum on the Fourteenth Amendment, and Northern voters came down squarely on the side of the Radicals. The Republicans elected 128 members to the House, against thirty-three Democrats, and retained their three-to-one edge in the Senate. In every state where a governorship was contested, the Republicans won; in every state other than Maryland where the legislature was up, the Republicans carried it.

The lame duck 39th Congress reassembled in Washington on December 3, 1866. Its term would expire March 3rd, and ordinarily the newly elected 40th Congress would not meet until the next December. But the Republicans were unwilling to allow so long an interval, lest President Johnson use the hiatus to undo their plans for Reconstruction.

As its first order of business the outgoing Congress broke precedent and enacted legislation calling the 40th Congress into session on March 4, 1867. That would ensure continuous legislative oversight of Reconstruction and limit President Johnson's ability to act independently. Congress then passed a District of Columbia bill enfranchising freedmen in the nation's capital and the first of three Reconstruction Acts placing the South under military government. All three measures became law over Johnson's veto. Finally, the president's power as Commander-in-Chief was curtailed through a rider attached to the Military Appropriations Bill. Henceforth, any orders Johnson might have for the army would have to be issued through Grant as general-in-chief, who, the rider specified, could not be removed without the Senate's consent.

II. President

The adoption of the Fifteenth Amendment to the Constitution completes the greatest civil change, and constitutes the most important political event that has occurred, since the nation came into life.

Ulysses S. Grant, March 30, 1870

Ulysses Grant was elected President of the United States on Nov. 3, 1868.[4] Three months later, both houses of Congress passed the Fifteenth Amendment to the United States Constitution, prohibiting federal and state governments from denying a citizen the right to vote based on that citizen's "race, color, or previous condition of servitude." After an intense national battle, lasting more than one year, the amendment was ratified and adopted on March 30, 1870.

During the next two years, armed with the authority of the 13th, 14th and 15th Amendments, Congress, with the full support of President Grant, enacted three "Enforcement Acts" to ensure compliance throughout the South to the policy of Reconstruction. These Acts were criminal codes which protected African-Americans' right to vote, to hold office, to serve on juries, and receive equal protection of laws. The Second Enforcement Act ("An Act to enforce the rights of citizens of the United States to vote in the several states of this union"), permitted federal oversight of local and state elections if any two citizens in a town with more than twenty thousand inhabitants desired it.

The Third Enforcement Act, aka the Ku Klux Klan Act, was drafted by the Grant White House and passed by Congress only at the personal insistence of the President. It made state officials liable in federal court for depriving anyone of civil rights or the equal protection of the laws. It further elevated a number of the KKK's intimidation tactics into federal offenses, authorized the President to call out the militia to suppress conspiracies against the operation of the national government, and prohibited those suspected of complicity in such conspiracies to serve on juries related to the Klan's ac-

Library of Congress

President Ulysses S. Grant, as photographed by Matthew Brady, sometime during his two terms. (1869-1877)

tivities. The Act also authorized the President to suspend the writ of *habeas corpus* if violence rendered efforts to suppress the Klan ineffective.[5]

At first the Congressional Republican leadership refused to support such sweeping legislation. On March 23, with his entire cabinet in attendance, Grant made a rare visit to Capitol Hill where he told the Republican legislators that "the Ku Klux Klan was attempting to reverse the decision at Appomattox....," and that there was "no other subject on which I would recommend legislation during the current session."

At the same time, also at Grant's request, Congress passed legislation—signed into law on Feb. 25, 1870—

---

4. In the Presidential election of 1868, out of 5,720,000 votes cast, Grant defeated the Copperhead Democrat Horatio Seymour by 306,000 votes. Because of the actions of the Union Army between 1865 and 1868, over 700,000 Southern Blacks voted in the election, and it is almost certain that it was their votes which made the difference for Grant.

5. In his second inaugural address, Grant called for another civil rights act. This resulted in a fourth Enforcement Act, aka the Civil Rights Act of 1875, which guaranteed African-Americans equal treatment in public accommodations, public transportation, and prohibited exclusion from jury service. Declared unconstitutional during the later Jim Crow Era, the Civil Rights Act of 1875 would be the last Civil Rights legislation enacted in the United States until the Eisenhower-era Civil Rights Act of 1957. In 1964, several of the original provisions of the 1875 Act would be included, almost verbatim, in the Civil Rights Act of 1964.

18   War Against Thermonuclear War

EIR   August 14, 2015

establishing the U.S. Justice Department. This was done explicitly to provide the Attorney General with greater resources to enforce the provisions of both the Enforcement Acts as well as the mandates of the 13th, 14th and 15th Amendments. Grant's second Attorney General, Amos T. Akerman, used these new capabilities to their fullest potential.

A Shooting War

Led by the Ku Klux Klan, a reign of terror was unleashed upon the South. Black schools were burned, teachers beaten, voters intimidated, and political opponents of both races kidnapped and killed. Hundreds of black soldiers, Freedmen's Bureau officials, and elected officials were

"The Louisiana Murders," an illustration from Harper's Weekly, *depicts the aftermath of the Colfax massacre of 1873, one of the most horrendous mass-murders of blacks in the Confederate guerrilla war during the Grant administrations.*

murdered outright. The Autumn elections in 1870 were particularly violent. In South Carolina, observers listed 227 "outrages" in one county, 118 in another, and 300 in a third. In North Carolina, Klan terrorism helped the Democrats recapture the state, electing five of seven congressmen. Attorney General Akerman, assisted by Union troops, began a sweeping prosecution of Klan members. In North Carolina, where army units sent by Grant helped apprehend suspects, hundreds of men were indicted. In northern Mississippi, where Klan violence was endemic, United States attorneys secured nearly 1,000 indictments in the early 1870s, and fully 55% of the cases resulted in conviction.

After a series of incidents in early May, Grant ordered troops in the South to take the field and help federal officials "arrest and break up bands of disguised night marauders." In October, when Akerman reported the situation in South Carolina out of control, Grant proclaimed "a condition of lawlessness" in nine upland counties, suspended the writ of *habeas corpus*, and rushed reinforcements to the state. With Akerman directing operations on the spot, United States marshals, assisted by squads of soldiers, made hundreds of arrests, forced an estimated 2,000 Klansmen to flee the state, and restored a semblance of order to the region. Throughout the South the Klan was put on the defensive. Federal grand juries returned more than 3,000 indictments in 1871. By 1872 Grant's willingness to bring the full legal and military authority of the Government

to bear had broken the Klan's back and produced a dramatic decline in violence in the South. The election of 1872 went off without a hitch. African-Americans voted in record numbers, with Union troops standing watch.

The military and judicial defeat of the Klan did not stop the violence. Other groups emerged. Perhaps the worst of these was The White League, founded in Louisiana in 1874 by Confederate veterans who had participated in the Colfax massacre in April 1873. Through violence, intimidation, and assassination, its members reduced Republican voting and contributed to the Democrats' taking over control of the Louisiana Legislature in 1876. Another group was The Red Shirts, founded originally in Mississippi in 1875, later becoming very active in both North and South Carolina. These were para-military groups, which combined murder and outright terrorism with electoral politics, their intent being to subjugate the blacks and drive both the national Army and the Republican Party out of the South.

The Colfax Massacre and its aftermath was a turning point in Reconstruction. Colfax was the county seat of Grant Parish, in Louisianna. On Easter Sunday, 1873, militia and freedmen loyal to the official government guarded the courthouse to protect county officers. They were attacked and overpowered by whites armed with rifles and light artillery. When the sun set, well over a hundred blacks were dead, many shot in cold blood after they had surrendered. A federal grand jury indicted seventy-two whites for their part in the massacre, nine were tried, and three were convicted. In 1875, the U.S. Supreme Court, in *United States v. Cruikshank*, overturned these convictions, ruling parts of the Enforcement Act of 1870 unconstitutional and limiting the power of the National Government to intervene to protect the rights of private citizens.

The violence escalated. In Coushatta, near Shreveport, the local White League murdered six Republican officeholders. In New Orleans, on September 14, police and black militia commanded by General Longstreet fought a pitched battle with 3,500 White Leaguers intent on seizing the statehouse and overturning the government. Longstreet, who was wounded in the fighting, lost eleven killed and sixty wounded, and the White League succeeded in storming the state offices and installing a rival Democratic government.

If Grant had been looking for an easy way out, he would have accepted the New Orleans *coup d'état*. Instead, he moved swiftly to suppress the revolt. On September 15, 1874, the day after the battle, Grant issued a Presidential Proclamation calling on the rebellious citizens to disperse within five days and submit to the duly elected state government. Five thousand troops and three gunboats were dispatched to New Orleans, resistance crumbled, and by September 17 the insurgency had been crushed.

On Christmas Eve 1874, President Grant sent a private wire to Sheridan in Chicago instructing him to undertake an immediate inspection of Louisiana and Mississippi and "ascertain the true condition of affairs." Sheridan was given what amounted to as a military blank check, and he was authorized to issue orders on the spot, and if he deemed it necessary, to assume command of the Division of the South. In effect, Grant was assuming personal responsibility for Louisiana, with Sheridan as his deputy.

The Louisiana legislature was set to convene January 4, 1875. Sheridan arrived a few days before. When the legislature convened on January 4, the Democrats forcibly seized control of the House and proceeded to seat the five Democratic claimants to the contested seats. In response, the Republican governor requested the army to evict the five Democrats, none of whom possessed the proper election credentials. Under Sheridan's direction, the five newly seated Democrats were forcibly ejected, at which point the remainder of the Democrats stalked out in protest. The Republicans then organized the House and elected a speaker.

That evening, Sheridan assumed command in New Orleans. The firestorm raged for a week. Sheridan was threatened with assassination, and in Washington, the Senate requested details of the situation. Grant replied on Jan. 13 with a blistering report detailing the atrocities in Louisiana and strongly defending Sheridan's actions:

The spirit of hatred and violence is stronger than law.... Lieutenant-General Sheridan was requested by me to go to Louisiana to observe and report. No party motives nor prejudices can reasonably be imputed to him; but honestly convinced by what he has seen and heard there, he has characterized the leaders of the White Leagues in severe terms and suggested summary modes of procedure against them, which ... if legal, would soon put an end to the troubles and disorders in that State.... To the extent that Congress has conferred power upon me to prevent it, neither Ku Klux Klans, White Leagues, nor any other associations using arms and violence can be permitted to govern any part of this country. (Message to the Senate, January 13, 1875)

For the last two years of his Administration, Grant stood watch over the South almost alone. His cabinet was uninterested, the Supreme Court had eviscerated the Fourteenth and Fifteenth Amendments, and the same group of "Liberal Republicans" who had attempted his defeat in the 1872 election were now condemning him and calling for an end to Reconstruction.[6] But Grant never wavered, and as in the Wilderness, he never stopped fighting.

Shortly after he left the Presidency, Grant reflected on the postwar period:

Looking back, over the whole policy of reconstruction, it seems to me that the wisest thing would have been to have continued for some time the military rule. That would have enabled the Southern people to pull themselves together and repair material losses. Military rule would have been just to all: the negro who wanted free-

---

6. This network included Horace Greeley, Edwin L. Godkin of *The Nation*, William Cullen Bryant of the *Evening Post*, James Russell Lowell and David A. Wells of the *North American Review*, Henry Adams together with most of the Adams Family, and Carl Schurz.

dom, the white man who wanted protection, the Northern man who wanted Union. As state after state showed a willingness to come into the Union, *not on their terms but upon ours*, I would have admitted them. The trouble about the military rule in the South was that our people (in the north) did not like it. It was not in accordance with our institutions. I am clear now that it would have been better to have postponed suffrage, reconstruction, State governments, for ten years, and held the South in a territorial condition. But we made our scheme, and must do what we can with it. Suffrage once given can never be taken away, and all that remains now is to make good that gift by protecting those that received it.

This painting by Robert Lindneux shows the "Trail of Tears," the forced march of the Southeastern Indian tribes, thousands to their death, mandated by Andrew Jackson's Indian Removal Act of 1830.

III. Another fight for the Human Soul

In April of 1869 President Grant stunned the nation once again when he appointed his longtime aide, Brigadier General Ely S. Parker, commissioner of Indian affairs.[7] Already, in his inaugural, Grant had spoken in heartfelt terms about the plight of Native Americans, and the implications of his appointment of Parker, a full-blooded chief of the Senecas and grand sachem of the Iroquois Confederacy, were undeniable. Already, between his election and inauguration, Grant had deployed Parker to explore with the Society of Friends the

possibility of employing Quakers as Indian agents, and by appointing Parker and enlisting the Quakers he moved quickly and aggressively to put in place what would soon be known as "Grant's Peace Policy" toward the Plains Indians.

Grant's policy was a revolution against what had been official U.S. policy since the administration of Thomas Jefferson, a policy which can only be characterized as "slow extermination." In 1803 Jefferson suggested relocating the Indians west of the Mississippi. Later, James Monroe proposed the Eastern Tribes be forced to remove to the region "between the present States and Territories and the Rocky Mountains." In 1830, at Andrew Jackson's urging, Congress passed the Indian Removal Act, leading to the forced ethnic cleansing of the Southeast, and the deaths of thousands of Creek, Cherokee, Choctaw, Seminole, and Chickasaw Indians along the infamous "Trail of Tears."

When Grant took office, he reversed 70 years of U.S. government policy. At that time, in 1869, the Great Plains seethed with unrest. Clashes with the western Indians had grown more frequent and more violent since 1862. Treaties with the Indians had not been honored, the tribes were becoming increasingly militant and settlers were clamoring for protection. The Jefferson/Jackson policy had been one of extermination against the

---

7. Ely Parker was also an accomplished engineer, lawyer, and soldier, who as a young man had been a director of work crews on the Erie Canal, served as resident engineer in charge of construction of the Chesapeake and Albemarle Canal linking Norfolk with Albemarle Sound in North Carolina, and then built lighthouses for the Treasury Department along the Great Lakes.

Indians, and many in 1869 expected Grant to act in similar fashion. The result would have been total war with tens of thousands of deaths. Grant abruptly changed direction. Rather than fight, he chose to make peace with the Plains Indians.

Quite simply, Grant believed that the Indians deserved better treatment. Unlike many of his military commanders, Grant believed that most of the problems on the frontier were attributable to the settlers.

Grant also believed Indian affairs had been consistently mishandled. "Most Indian wars have grown out of mismanagement of the Bureau [of Indian Affairs]," he wrote Sheridan in disgust on Christmas Eve, 1868. Above all, Grant believed Indians should be treated as individuals, and that they should be afforded the opportunity to become citizens as quickly as possible. Grant's conciliatory approach to Indian affairs was shocking to many Americans.

Grant's messages to Congress and the American people pleaded the Indian cause with an intensity rarely encountered in official communications:

> *Wars of extermination . . . are demoralizing and wicked. Our superiority should make us lenient toward the Indian. The wrongs inflicted upon him should be taken into account and the balance placed to his credit.* (First Annual Message to Congress, December 6, 1869)
>
> *A system which looks to the extinction of a race is too horrible for a nation to adopt without entailing upon itself the wrath of all Christendom and engendering in the citizens a disregard for human life and the rights of others, dangerous to society.*
>
> *Can not the Indian be made a useful and pro-*

Library of Congress

President Grant (second from left) shakes hands with Red Cloud, the chief of the Oglala Sioux, during his visit to Washington in 1870.

> *ductive member of society? If the effort is made in good faith, we will stand better before the civilized nations of the earth and our own consciences for having made it.* (Second Inaugural, March 4, 1873.)
>
> *I do not believe our Creator ever placed the different races on this earth with a view of having the strong exert all his energies in exterminating the weaker.*

As in Reconstruction, Congress, at first, gave Grant what he wanted. $5 million was appropriated for food and supplies for the Western Tribes, and another $2 million to enable the President to secure peace. The President was authorized to appoint a ten-person Board of Indian Commissioners. That Board would later issue a report recommending the concentration of the Indians on small reservations, abolition of the treaty system, and immediate citizenship for the Five Civilized Tribes in the Indian Territory (Creek, Cherokee, Choctaw, Chickasaw, and Seminole). Above all, the board recommended that Indian agents and district superintendents be selected on the basis of moral and business qualifications, without reference to political affiliation.

Grant also initiated what became known as his "Quaker Policy," enlisting hundreds of Quakers as Indian agents. When enough representatives of the Society of Friends could not be found to fill all of the posts, Grant replaced the remaining Indian agents with army officers on active duty, men he was confident he could count on to carry out orders without reaching into the till.

Grant's peace policy was almost destroyed when, on January 23, 1870, elements of the 2nd Cavalry, seeking to punish renegade Piegan warriors (the Piegans were a subset of the Blackfeet tribe), fell upon and destroyed a Piegan village along the banks of the Marias River in northern Montana. This was a defenseless tribal village, made up of mostly women and children, many suffering the final stages of smallpox. One hundred seventy-three Indians were killed; all but fifteen were women and children. Fifty of the casualties were children under twelve, many in their parents' arms. Northern newspapers labeled it "a sickening slaughter," and a "national disgrace."

Despite this incident, Grant's policy was succeeding. The White House received a message that Red Cloud, the mighty chief of the Oglala Sioux, wanted to meet the "Great Father." The meeting was arranged, and Red Cloud, together with a group of other Chiefs, met with the President. Following this meeting, for the remainder of his life, Red Cloud never again took up arms against the United States. Another of the Chiefs, Spotted Tail, said he was for peace, but the government had not reciprocated. Grant acted swiftly. The following day the War Department issued orders to all military commanders in the West: "When lands are secured to the Indians by treaty against the occupation by whites, the military commander should keep intruders off by military force if necessary."

From Washington the Sioux chiefs traveled to New York. On June 16, 1870, the delegation made a triumphant appearance before a capacity crowd at Cooper Union. A packed auditorium heard Red Cloud deliver an eloquent indictment of past policy. "The riches we have in this world, Secretary Cox said truly, we cannot take with us to the next world. Then I wish to know why agents are sent out to us who do nothing but rob us and get the riches of this world away from us?" Red Cloud's description of the wrongs suffered by the Indians held the audience spellbound. A reporter from *The Nation* noted that the emotional effect "was comparable to the public recital of a fugitive slave in former years."

Peace with Red Cloud and the Oglala Sioux was a major achievement. Other breakthroughs followed. In December 1870 the Five Civilized Tribes, meeting in Okmulgee, about forty miles south of Tulsa, approved a constitution and bill of rights for a territorial government and a future Indian state. Grant immediately forwarded the documents to Congress and urged quick approval.

But the Indian proposal for territorial government provided for more independence than Congress cared for. Amendments were proposed giving final authority over legislation and appointments to the government in Washington, and at that point the Native Americans backed away. The railroads, with a huge stake in rights-of-way across Indian land, also opposed territorial status. As a result, the most serious effort to extend citizenship to the Native Americans in Indian territory was never realized.

In the Southwest, Major General Oliver Otis Howard rode unarmed and alone into Cochise's stronghold in the Dragoon Mountains of Arizona and convinced the legendary chief of the Chiricahua Apaches to move onto a nearby reservation. Howard's bold gambit brought peace to a large portion of the Southwest, and for the first time since 1861 Cochise's warriors posed no danger to the settlers. Oliver Otis Howard was typical of a number of senior officers in the West who supported Grant's peace policy. Known as "humanitarian generals," they shared the President's view that relations with the Indians should be based on honesty, justice, and eventual assimilation.

Perhaps the greatest of the humanitarian generals was George Crook. A West Point classmate of Sheridan's, Crook had turned Jubal Early's flank at Fisher's Hill and later commanded a cavalry division in the Army of the Potomac. He served more than thirty years in the West and worked assiduously to make the Apaches self-sufficient. He fought tenaciously against unscrupulous government functionaries both within the military and without. When Crook died in 1890, he was eulogized as a tower of strength for those who worked for Indian equality. Red Cloud said, "General Crook came, and he, at least, never lied to us. His words gave people hope." Against the advice of many people, Grant never ceased in his support for his humanitarian generals, and despite many setbacks and efforts to sabotage relations with the Indians, Grant maintained his Peace Policy until the day he left office.

IV. Against Empire

The Centennial International Exhibition of 1876, the first official World's Fair in the United States, was held in Philadelphia, Pennsylvania, from May 10 to Nov. 10, 1876. Bells rang all over Philadelphia to signal the Centennial's opening. The opening ceremony was attended by U.S. President Ulysses Grant and his wife and Brazilian Emperor Dom Pedro II and his wife. The opening ceremony ended in Machinery Hall with Grant

wikimedia.org

President Grant and the Brazilian Emperor Dom Pedro stand before the huge Corliss Steam Engine, as they inaugurate the 1876 Centennial Exhibition in Philadelphia.

and Dom Pedro turning on the Corliss Steam Engine which powered most of the other machines at the Exposition. The science, the industry, the might of the American Republic was on display for the entire world to witness.

One year later, on May 17, 1877, Ulysses Grant, now ex-President, together with his wife, aides, and other family members, left Philadelphia on a two-and-one-half year long circumnavigation of the earth, a world tour which would take them through Europe, Africa, Asia, and across the Pacific. During this trip, Grant visited more countries, saw more people, and conversed with more kings, diplomats, and world rulers than any other individual in history up to that time.

Ignored in all history books and relegated by most historians to the status of a retirement pleasure trip, Grant's World Tour was his final, profound intervention on behalf of the American Republic and against the power and principles of the British Empire.

It must be understood that Grant, at this time, was a legendary figure, the Hero of Appomattox, the victor of the world's greatest war since the fall of Napoleon, and the two-term American President who had vanquished Southern slavery. He also personified and represented the marvel of modern American technological and industrial power.

In England, Grant and his wife were Queen Victoria's houseguests at Windsor Castle. In France, Marshal MacMahon, president of the Third Republic, spent days at Grant's side. In Italy, he talked with Leo XIII, the reformist Pope, and dined with King Umberto. In Russia, Czar Alexander discussed the future of the Plains Indians at length with the ex-President. Later, in Egypt, China, Japan, and many other nation's Grant was given a hero's welcome.

In Berlin, no sooner had Grant arrived than Chancellor Bismarck sent his card, requesting a private meeting. The former president immediately returned the courtesy, and a meeting was arranged for four o'clock that afternoon. John Russell Young, later Librarian of Congress, accompanied Grant on the trip and here he relates the impact of Grant on Bismarck and their discussion of the Civil War:

Bismarck began by stating to Grant, "You are so happily placed in America that you need fear no wars. What always seemed so sad to me about your last great war was that you were fighting your own people. That is always so terrible in wars so very hard."

"But it had to be done," said the General.

"Yes," said the prince, "you had to save the Union just as we had to save Germany."

"Not only save the Union, but destroy slavery," answered the General.

"I suppose, however, the Union was the real sentiment, the dominant sentiment," said the prince.

"In the beginning, yes," said the General; "But as soon as slavery fired upon the flag, it was felt, we all felt, even those who did not object to slaves, that slavery must be destroyed. We felt that it was a stain to the Union that men should be bought and sold like cattle."

"I suppose if you had a large army in the beginning, the war would have ended in a much shorter time."

"We might well have had no war at all," said the General, "but we cannot tell. Our war had many strange features, there were many things which seemed odd enough at the time, but which now seem Providential. If we had had a large army, as it was then constituted, it might have gone with the South. In fact, the Southern feeling in the army among high officers was so strong that when the war broke out, the army dissolved. We had no army. Then we had to organize one. A great commander like Sherman or Sheridan even then might have organized an army and put down the rebellion in six months or a year, or, at the farthest, two years. But that would have saved slavery, perhaps, and slavery meant the germs of new rebellion. There had to be an end to slavery. Then we were fighting an enemy with whom we could not make peace. We had to destroy him. No convention, no treaty was possible only destruction."

"It was a long war," said the prince, "and a great work well done and I suppose it means a long peace."

"I believe so," said the General.

From Berlin, Grant traveled to Scandinavia, then to Russia to meet with Emperor Alexander II, and with Russian Foreign Minister Gorchakov. Alexander II had been an ally of Lincoln during the Civil War and, during the war, had sent Russian ships to both the East and the West Coast of the United States, signaling to the British that if they were to enter the war on the side of the Confederacy, the Union side would not be without its allies. Visiting Kronstadt, Grant also met some of the sailors who had been on the Russian ships during the Civil War.

In Grant's discussions with Alexander, the Czar asked him many questions about his policy with the Indians, explaining that as the head of an empire with many different ethnic groups, he desired to learn from Grant how these differences could be overcome through diplomacy, rather than war. When he was leaving, Alexander said: "Since the foundation of your Government, relations between Russia and America have been of the friendliest character, and as long as I live nothing shall be spared to continue this friendship."

Much of Grant's agenda in Germany, France, and northern Europe was spent on examining industrial areas. As a clear sign of his personal interest in technology and manufactures, Grant spent a full day in March 1878 at the Paris Exposition examining state-of-the-art machinery.

The record of Grant's conversations with European

en.wikipedia.org

Chancellor Otto von Bismarck in 1873, one of the many world leaders whom former President Grant met and advised during his world tour in the late 1870s.

leaders, particularly in his repeated stress on the issues of slavery and the American Indians, demonstrates an undeniable conscious intent to convey the essence of the American Constitutional Republic to these leaders, to communicate the meaning of what it means to be an American citizen.

From Russia, the Grants went back to France, and on to the Iberian Peninsula, Egypt and the pyramids, the Holy Land, Constantinople, and Athens, which required another several months. Much of this time the Grants spent in Egypt, visiting and studying archaeological sites, museums and all aspects of Egypt's 7,000 year history.[8] From the Mediterranean Grant sailed through the Suez canal, which had opened only eight years earlier, to the Red Sea, India, and the Orient. Most of 1879 was moving through Bombay, Delhi, the Straits of Malacca, Singapore, Siam (Thailand), Hong Kong, Canton, Shanghai, Tientsin and Peking, and Japan.

Confronting the Empire

It was in Asia that Grant made his most powerful intervention on the world stage. Throughout his travels in Asia Grant was appalled by the racist attitude of the Westerners he found living there. Visiting India, Grant commented, "The British did not come to India to leave money behind, but to take it away." Later, in China he remarked, "The course of the average minister, consul, and merchant in this country towards the native is much

---

8. Grant spent hundreds of hours examining the architectural masterpieces, art galleries, and museums along his route. In Paris, he spent days in the Louvre. In Rome, he browsed the Vatican library, and spent long sessions in the Sistine Chapel admiring the frescoes of Michelangelo and the Coronation of the Virgin by Raphael. In Florence, his first stop was the Uffizi Gallery, where he spent a full day. Young reported that the General devoted the following day to the Pitti Palace, taking in the beauty of more priceless paintings by Rubens, Raphael, Titian, and Veronese. In Berlin, it was Museum Island on the Spree, the famous Egyptian collection at the Altes Museum, and another of the world's great collections of old masters at the *Gemäldegalerie*.

like the course of the former slave owner towards the freedman when the latter attempts to think for himself in matters of choice of candidates."

Upon his arrival in China, Grant was greeted with an unprecedented twenty-one gun salute. During his stay he held numerous meetings with Li Hung-Chang, the great viceroy of the Middle Kingdom, whom Grant compared to Bismarck. In their discussions, Grant underlined the importance of the construction of railroads and similar infrastructure for strengthening the Chinese nation.

The Grants arrived in Japan on July 4, 1879 and stayed for three months. Their landing took place at Nagasaki. Later, in Tokyo, after the festivities and the banquets, he was granted a personal audience with Emperor Meiji, who was also eager to speak with him. During this and later meetings with leading members of the Japanese government, Grant was extraordinarily pointed in his warnings against the British Empire. He told the Emperor:

> Nothing has been of more interest to me than the study of the growth of European and foreign influence in Asia. When I was in India, I saw what England had done with that empire, but since I left India, I have seen things that made my blood boil, in the way the European powers attempt to degrade the Asiatic nations. I would not believe such a policy possible. It seems to have no other aim than the extinction of the independence of the Asiatic nations. On that subject I feel strongly, and in all that I have written to friends at home, I have spoken strongly. I feel so about Japan and China.

Grant also warned against taking foreign loans. Using the example of how Egypt and Turkey had been put under the thumb of Britain through such loans, Grant explained:

> There is nothing a nation should avoid as much as owing money abroad.... You are doubtless aware that some nations are very desirous to loan money to weaker nations whereby they might establish their supremacy and exercise undue influence over them. They lend money to gain political power. They are ever seeking the opportunity to loan. They would be glad, therefore, to see Japan and China, which are the only

A drawing of President Grant's meeting with the Emperor of Japan in the Emperor's summer-house, during his 1879 visit to that nation.

> nations in Asia that are even partially free from foreign rule or dictation, at war with each other so that they might loan them on their terms and dictate to them the internal policy which they should pursue.

Grant's relationship with the Japanese government had actually begun earlier, during his Presidency, with the 1871-1872 tour of the United States by the Iwakura Embassy. Composed of leading figures from the Japanese government, and led by Ambassador Iwakura, the Embassy spent two years touring the United States, visiting steel mills, locomotive factories, machine tool plants, universities, farms, and other productive facilities. In Washington, D.C., they visited Congress, the Supreme Court, and the Library of Congress, and on March 14 the Embassy held a formal reception at Arlington House Hotel, with President Grant and over 1000 of Washington's most prominent political, commercial, and social movers in attendance. On April 1 the Embassy had another dinner with President Grant, which also included Vice President Schuyler Colfax and twenty-eight heads of the U.S. military and civilian affairs.

A month before his departure from Japan, Grant wrote a letter to a friend in America, wherein he said:

> The progress they have made in the last twelve years is almost incredible. They have now Military and Naval Academies, Colleges, Engineering schools, schools of science, and free schools, for male and female, as thoroughly organized, and on as high a basis of instruction, as any country in the world. This is marvelous when the treatment their people—and all eastern peoples—receive at the hands of the average foreigner residing among them is considered. I have never been so struck with the heartlessness of Nations as well as individuals as since coming to the East. But the day of retribution is sure to come.

Grant sailed for San Francisco on the City of Tokio steamer, Sept. 3, 1879. The imperial cavalry escorted him to the palace, where Emperor Meiji and the Empress were waiting to say goodbye. The route from Tokyo was lined with cheering multitudes waving American and Japanese flags. At the Admiralty Wharf, Grant was greeted by the Japanese naval command, the fleet riding at anchor in the distance. A navy band broke into "Hail Columbia," fireworks lit the sky, and the Admiralty barge, festooned with color, moved out into the harbor, carrying the general to his steamer. The City of Tokio, the largest steamer on the Pacific run, got underway, convoyed to the open seas by a Japanese man-of-war, the imperial cabinet drawn up on deck. One by one, as Grant's vessel passed, the naval ships in the harbor bellowed a twenty-one-gun salute, cheering crewmen aloft in the rigging and manning the yards. As Mount Fujiyama faded in the distance, the accompanying Japanese man-of-war turned homeward and fired a final salvo in salute.

EIRNS/Stuart Lewis

"Let us have peace," is the motto on Grant's Tomb in Riverside Park, Manhattan, shown here.

V. War against War

Upon his return to the United States, Grant held discussions with Secretary of State William Evarts. He urged the United States to issue a Monroe Doctrine proclamation, short of an alliance, as a statement of principles committing the United States to long-term cooperation with Japan and China, a statement that would send a clear message to the British, as well as to China and Japan, regarding U.S. intentions. As he had noted, a war between the two countries would be devastating, and it would result in the opening-up of both nations to European nations eager to gobble up the pieces as China fell apart.

On learning in 1881 that China was intent on building railroads to unite the country, an issue which Grant had recommended during his talks with China's Prince Kong, he wrote to Li Hongzhang:

> Just the day before I was obliged to leave New York City in order to connect with the steamer now about to depart, I learned that your great country was contemplating the building of four great trunk lines of rail roads. I was delighted to hear this, and had I not been obliged to hurry off could have made it my duty and pleasure to have seen the Chinese representatives to our country to offer my assistance in any way that I might be

useful. You no doubt remember the conversations we had on the importance of railroads to develop the resources of the country; to give employment to the millions, and to give strength to a country against an outside enemy.

Grant also expressed a willingness to help in whatever way he could to make this a reality. "If China contemplates what I hope she does—the building of railroads—I would advise an examination of our system before adopting any other," Grant wrote.

I think we build railroads faster than any other country, build them quite as well, and build better locomotives and other rolling stock. For civil engineers, especially those engaged in the construction of rail-roads and all connected with them, the American engineer is unsurpassed. Should a foreign loan be required it can be effected in the United States, through an American syndicate as well as elsewhere. I repeat: If I can help China in matters of internal improvements, either in suggesting persons for employment in laying out roads, building them, or running them after being built; to construct and superintend the necessary work shops for repairs; or in suggesting parties here to negotiate any loan that may be wanted, I will be glad to render such service.

* * *

And there we have the man, from Appomattox, through Reconstruction, his eight-year Presidency, and his final intervention against the British Empire in Asia. His commitment to human equality and *human development*, as exemplified in his ten-year battle for justice in both the South and among the Indians of the American West is unparalleled in the history of our Nation.

Most compelling, Grant understood that it was this quality of what America represented—of what had been won in the 1861-1877 years—that provided the basis through which friendships could be built with other nations and peoples, capable of defeating the anti-human policies of empire and securing the future for all nations. His was always a *Peace-winning strategy*, and if it had fully succeeded, the later events of the Nineteenth Century, together with the World War of 1914, never would have occurred.

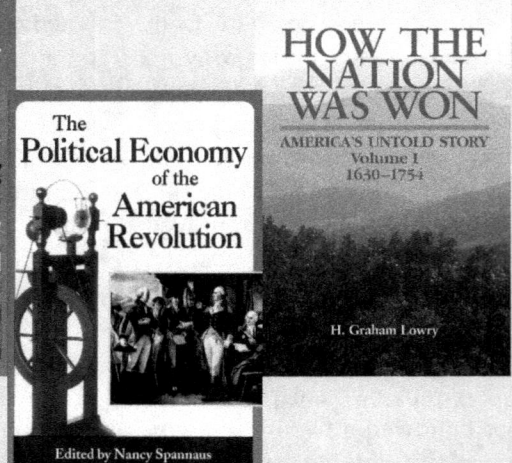

Every Day Counts In Today's Showdown To Save Civilization

That's why you need *EIR*'s **Daily Alert Service**, a strategic overview compiled with the input of Lyndon LaRouche, and delivered to your email 5 days a week.

For example: On July 27 Lyndon LaRouche identified this August as a period of maximum danger that President Barack Obama will launch provocations against Russia that could lead to the thermonuclear extinction of mankind.

EIR's July 28 Alert featured LaRouche's evaluation, along with critical intelligence on the Russian strategic doctrine. Throughout the rest of the week, the Alert has pointed to the way Hillary Clinton's exposure of Obama could interrupt Obama's war drive—as well as updates on the worsening threat.

This is intelligence you need to act on, if we are going to survive as a nation and a species. Can you really afford to be without it?

The Suez and Nicaragua Canals Reshape the World Ocean

by Dennis Small

Aug. 10—On Aug. 6, 2015, Egyptian President Abdel Fattah el-Sisi, at a ceremony in Ismailia, Egypt, inaugurated the New Suez Canal, one of the most significant global infrastructure projects undertaken and completed on the planet in the last 100 years, and an enterprise brought to fruition in a stunning one year from inception to completion. President el-Sisi proudly proclaimed that "Egypt is a great country and has a civilization of 7,000 years," adding that the New Suez Canal is "Egypt's new gift for humanity."

Gen. el-Sisi chose to open the celebration in military uniform, traveling on the 150-year-old Presidential yacht *El-Mahroussa*, which was the first ship to cross the original Suez Canal when it was opened in 1869. And by his side was a nine-year-old cancer patient, Omar Salah, who had expressed his dream of meeting Egypt's president and attending the inauguration of the New Suez Canal. President el-Sisi told the gathered multitude that "the Egyptian state is determined ... to achieve the aspirations of its sons."

It is hard to know how many of those present were reminded of the refrain, well-known to most Americans, "Give me your tired, your poor, your huddled masses yearning to breathe free," from the Emma Lazarus poem engraved on the pedestal of the Statue of Liberty. That statue now sits in New York Harbor, but it was originally designed by French sculptor Frédéric-Auguste Bartholdi in 1869 for the then-newly-inaugurated Suez Canal.

Xinhua/MENA
Egyptian President Abdel Fattah el-Sisi, joined by a young Egyptian boy, at the ceremony opening the New Suez Canal August 6.

A Strategic Victory

Many prominent world leaders were present in Ismailia on Aug. 6, including French President François Hollande, Russian Prime Minister Dmitri Medvedev, Greek Prime Minister Alexis Tsipras, German Vice Chancellor Sigmar Gabriel, and heads of government and cabinet-level officials from dozens of other nations—not including the United States. President Barack Obama only saw fit to send the American ambassador in Cairo, a boorish diplomatic insult from the Administration that had tried to sink Egypt into chaos and warfare, by putting in power and supporting the pro-terrorist Muslim Brotherhood government of Mohamed Morsi, who nearly destroyed the country during his 2012-2013 reign.

Obama, at London's behest, had tried to turn Egypt

into another Libya, as part of their broader drive for thermonuclear confrontation with Russia and China. Instead, they were surprised and stymied by the 2013 popular revolution which overthrew Morsi and put Gen. el-Sisi in power. That set the clock back significantly in their race for global warfare.

And then the el-Sisi government proceeded to announce, launch, and execute the construction of the New Suez Canal at breakneck speed, completing in exactly one year what the government itself had originally posed as a three-year project. By demanding that the job be done in one year, el-Sisi unleashed a mission-oriented sense of creativity and "can do" optimism in the Egyptian population which made the seemingly impossible, achievable.

As one of the Egyptian engineers working on the project, Ali el-Kholy, put it in an interview included in an Aug. 4 *Nile TV* documentary on the project: "This canal is not just for us or for our children. It's for all coming generations. We will die, but it shall live on for hundreds of years, for our children, grandchildren, and great-grandchildren."

Not surprisingly, the full $8.4 billion cost of the New Suez Canal project was financed entirely with domestic resources, mobilized with national bonds sold only to Egyptian citizens *in one week.*

Speeding up the timetable also meant that the British Empire and their Obama stooge didn't even have time to realize what was happening and regroup, before the project was completed. As Lyndon LaRouche commented Aug. 7:

"Egypt was under attack, a massive attack; and that massive attack forced Egypt to accelerate the development of the two stages that were intended on this thing. And that was what forced them to pre-empt the situation by accelerating the rate of creation. In other words, they took what would be three years and reduced it to one; and by doing that, they crushed the options of the enemy."

LaRouche pointed to the significance of these developments:

"What's happened with the new canal way by Egypt, has now changed the whole planet. There are no longer several oceans: There's now one ocean. And the Atlantic Ocean and the Pacific Ocean are all opened up to the same thing."

"The canal in Egypt has opened up the world," La-

John Grigaitis
The Egyptian government staged the grand march from Verdi's Aida in honor of opening the New Suez Canal. Here, a performance of the opera by the Michigan Opera Theatre in May 2013.

Rouche continued, "so that you no longer have an Atlantic nation as opposed to an Asian nation. Everything's going to change suddenly as a result of what happened ... a successful accomplishment of changing the whole character of maritime trade throughout the whole planet. Because the whole planet is now open, with the Nicaraguan thing [the Nicaragua Grand Inter-Oceanic Canal] added in there, and this; it's all one thing now."

LaRouche summarized the strategic impact: "Reorganize the world! We have an excellent thing that just happened in Egypt.... They have opened up the possibility of development of the whole world, in various categories."

The World Ocean

Economic development *per se* is a *casus belli* as far as the British are concerned, both because it provides nations and peoples with an alternative to their dying system, but more fundamentally, because it is rooted in, and fosters, a concept of man as a creative species, a concept which threatens the British Empire's very existence: it is the ultimate weapon to win the war against the British Empire's war drive.

All the more so when development occurs in a location such as the Suez Canal. The British and French had owned the original Suez Canal until it was nationalized by Egypt in 1956, with the backing of U.S. President Dwight Eisenhower. The British thereby lost control of one of the key international maritime "chokepoints," as British geopolitics likes to describe such geographic-

FIGURE 1
The Suez, Kra and Nicaragua Canals and the World Land-Bridge

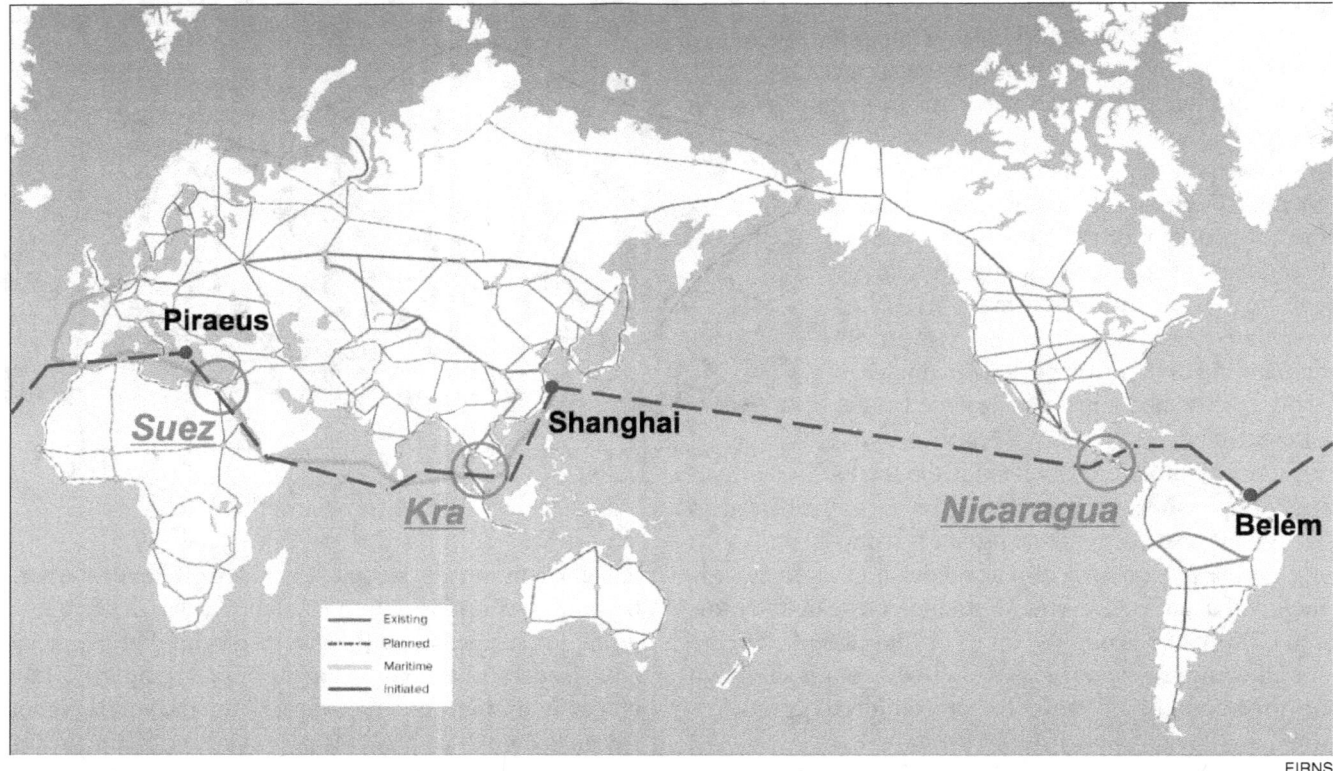

EIRNS

When added to the global system of transport corridors, land and sea, which are underway with the Chinese New Silk Road, Maritime Silk Road, and the World Land-Bridge projects, these three canals will create a whole new level of global connectivity: basically, there will now be one world ocean, one continent.

economic locations.

The New Suez Canal, as impressive as it is, is not a stand-alone project. Along with the Nicaragua Grand Inter-Oceanic Canal, scheduled for completion before 2020, and the Kra Canal in Thailand, long-designed and on the books, but which is still only under consideration, it will completely transform man's economic relationship to the world ocean. Conceived in conjunction with the World Land-Bridge (see **Figure 1**), whose high-speed rail lines will similarly link the continents into a single land-mass, humanity's relationship with the entire biosphere will be redefined: Man's planet Earth will truly become "One Ocean, One Continent," within the domain of the Solar and Galactic principles shaping its development.

The just-completed New Suez Canal project involved deepening and widening the existing canal along 37 kilometers of its total length of 193 km, as well as constructing an entirely new, parallel canal along 35 kilometers of the route. These 72 kilometers of new projects now allow two-way traffic along most of the route, shortening transit time from 18 hours to 11 hours on average, and doubling the number of ships that are able to cross through the canal, from 49 to 97 per day. The New Suez Canal can handle super-large cargo ships, with a maximum loaded weight of 240,000 DWT (deadweight tons). This is large enough to handle the very largest of today's container ships, and all but the ultra-large oil tankers and dry bulk carriers.

The New Suez Canal vastly shortens shipping distances and times to Europe from the booming Asian markets of China, India, etc., especially if the Greek port of Piraeus is expanded to become a principal port for much of these European imports and exports, with deep-water facilities and high-speed rail links extending into Europe. This is a major infrastructure project which the Chinese are avidly pursuing with the Greek government.

The Canal expansion is only the first stage of a much broader development project that the Egyptian government has undertaken, which includes: major expansion of Port Said and Port Suez; building a technology center in Ismailia; land reclamation; building industrial parks; constructing a half-dozen rail and road tunnels under the canal; major city building; and so on.

The BRICS nations, especially China and Russia, are playing a major role in these projects. In an interview with *Al-Ahram* during his visit for the inauguration of the Canal, Russian Prime Minister Dmitri Medvedev emphasized that "creating a Russian industrial zone in the Suez Canal could be the first step in this project. Nuclear power engineering is a strategic area of Russian-Egyptian cooperation. I'm not overstating it. Russia is willing to help Egypt become a regional leader in the nuclear industry."

Grand Strategy

The Nicaragua Grand Inter-Oceanic Canal, which will be built by the Nicaraguan government and the Chinese company HKND, is a great infrastructure project on an even larger scale than the New Suez Canal. Some 510 million cubic meters of earth were excavated for the New Suez Canal; the Nicaraguan project will move some 5 *billion* cubic meters—ten times more! The Nicaraguan Canal will connect the Atlantic and Pacific Oceans by cutting through the isthmus of Central America—another one of those historic British geopolitical chokepoints. It will complement the current Panama Canal, which has been open since 1914, but is now woefully inadequate for both the size of modern ships and the volume of international trade.

The current "Panamax" (maximum size of a ship that can pass through the Panama Canal) is about 5,000 TEU (twenty-foot equivalent units—the international standard used to measure container ship capacity). The largest container ships in the world are now 19,000 TEU and more. Even with the expansion of the Panama Canal that is now underway with the addition of two

TABLE 1

Comparison of Panama, Suez, Kra, and Nicaragua Canals

	Current Panama Canal	Expanded Panama Canal	Original Suez Canal	New Suez Canal	Kra Canal	Nicaragua Canal
Date in Service	(1914)	(2016)	(1869)	(2015)	proposed	(2019)
Length (km)	77	77	193	193	103	278
Maximum size (TEU)	5,000	13,000	14,000	20,000	25,000	25,000
Maximum size (thousand DWT)	65	180	200	280	400	400
Ships/day	30	60	49	97	(NA)	25
Transit time (hours)	8-10	8-10	18	11	8	30
Estimated cost (billions $)	(NA)	5.3	(NA)	8.4	20	50
Excavation/dredging (millions m3)	140	120	273	510	4,000	5,000

Sources: EIR, HKND, pancanal.com, suezcanal.gov.eg

new, larger locks (scheduled for completion in 2016), the Panama Canal will only be able to handle 13,000-TEU ships. The Nicaragua Grand Inter-Oceanic Canal will dwarf that, handling ships twice that size, of up to 25,000 TEU, along its 278 kilometer route (see **Table 1**).

Exemplary of the physical-economic impact this will have is the case of Brazil's huge (and growing) iron ore exports to China. At the end of 2014, the Brazilian government announced that it plans to increase its output of iron ore by 50% over the next five years, and has therefore placed orders with various Chinese and South Korean shipbuilders for 35 new cargo ships with a maximum capacity of some 400,000 dead-weight tons (DWT) each—way more than current cargo ships can handle. These ships will be too large to go through the expanded Panama Canal, and even the New Suez Canal. But they can be handled by the Nicaragua Grand Inter-Oceanic Canal. That westward route from Brazil, through the Nicaragua Canal, to China is about 10% shorter than the eastward maritime route currently taken from Brazil, across the Atlantic, around South Africa's Cape of Good Hope, to China.

But not all is clear sailing with the Nicaragua Grand Inter-Oceanic Canal. The British Empire has made it abundantly clear that it will do everything possible to make sure that this project never materializes, including mobilizing its environmentalist and indigenist shock troops, as well as financial and other forms of irregular warfare. A recent issue of the London *Econo-*

FIGURE 2

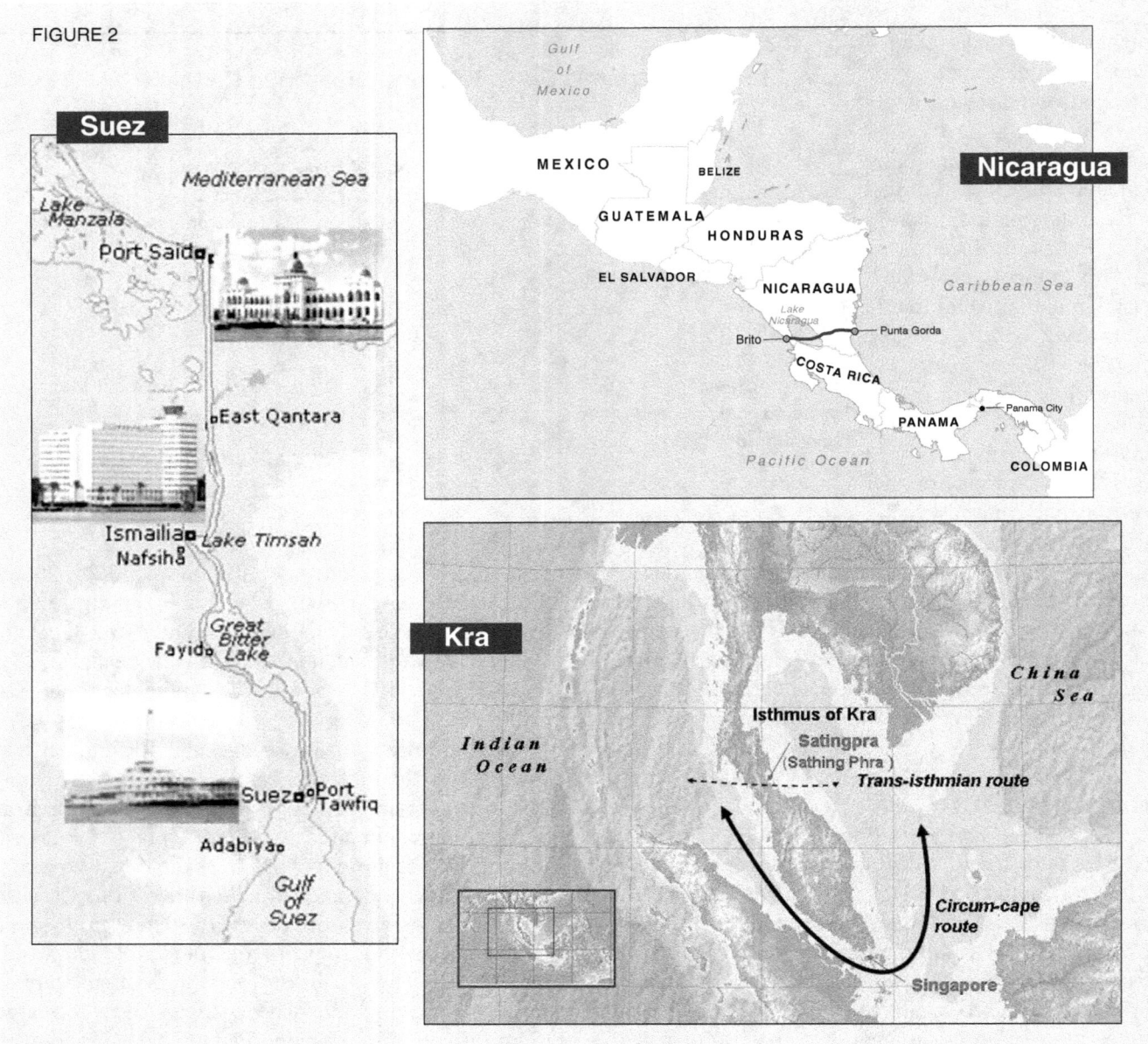

mist magazine described the Nicaraguan Canal as "surely one of the world's most improbable infrastructure projects, a pharaonic enterprise." The magazine then promised that "environmentalists will try to block it every step of the way."

It was thus of great strategic significance that Nicaraguan Vice President Moisés Omar Halleslevens participated in the ceremony inaugurating the New Suez Canal on Aug. 6; that he there met with Egyptian President el-Sisi; and that he received Egypt's strong support for the Nicaraguan project, including plans for the two countries' respective canal commissions to meet on a regular basis.

Egypt Did It, and So Will We!

The spokesman for the Nicaraguan Canal Commission, engineer Telémaco Talavera, spoke to *EIR* on Aug. 7, the day after the New Suez Canal was inaugurated, to express his congratulations and optimism. His basic message was: Egypt did it, and so will we!

Talavera called Egypt's canal "a great achievement, not only for Egypt, but in fact for the world ... as the Nicaraguan Canal will also be." Talavera added that the opening of the New Suez Canal "comes at a good time; many people didn't think it would be possible to achieve what was done with the Suez Canal in such a short period of time, just as today there are people who don't believe in the Nicaraguan Canal, or don't want it to become a reality."

Talavera noted that "the Egyptian President [el-Sisi] said, not only in a private meeting [with the Nicaraguan Vice President], not only at the inauguration of the canal, that he also celebrated Nicaragua's initiative and drive, and he offered all his help for the construction of the Nicaraguan Canal as well."

Talavera added: "We all know that the world's population has grown greatly and that it keeps growing. Exports and imports of products and goods are also growing, and so does the need to shorten distances, to reduce financial costs, to reduce environmental costs.... We are prepared to make that dream, that necessity, a reality." He concluded: "We celebrate this great triumph, not only for Egypt, but for the world, as we also celebrate the expansion of the Panama Canal and what will be an extraordinary project for the world, the Nicaraguan Canal, which is underway."

The Kra Canal: A 225-Year Wait

Add into the picture the long-planned Kra Canal in Thailand, which provides a direct shipping route from China and other Asian nations into the Indian Ocean and points west—by-passing the overcrowded Strait of Malacca, yet another British chokepoint—and you begin to get a picture of how these three great projects are already reshaping man's relationship to the world ocean.

Today, some 30% of all world trade uses the Strait of Malacca, which on average sees the passage of 210 ships per day, with a maximum size of 210,000 DWT (deadweight tons).

The Kra Canal would shorten shipping distances between the South China Sea and the Indian Ocean by over 1,000 kilometers, and allow the passage of ships of 400,000 DWT or more. Note that this geographic region of the planet—encompassing China, India, Japan, and the populous nations of Southeast Asia—is home to about *half* of the human race.

The optimal route and configuration for this canal would be a two-lane, sea-level, 103 kilometer route, whose excavation of some four billion cubic meters of earth would be significantly sped up by the use of peaceful nuclear explosives (PNE). It would be capable of handling the world's largest cargo ships, in the same range as the Nicaragua Grand Inter- Oceanic Canal.

Some form of Kra Canal project has been under consideration since the late Eighteenth Century. It was strongly promoted back in the 1980s by pro-development forces in Japan, centered around the Mitsubishi Research Institute, by interests in China, and by Lyndon LaRouche's international movement. In October 1983, *EIR* and the Fusion Energy Foundation (FEF), both founded by LaRouche, held a conference in Bangkok, co-sponsored by Thailand's Ministry of Transportation and the Global Infrastructure Fund (GIF), part of Japan's Mitsubishi Research Institute, promoting the construction of a sea-level canal across the Isthmus of Kra in southern Thailand.

At that conference, LaRouche remarked: "The prospect of establishing a sea-level waterway through the Isthmus of Thailand ought to be seen not only as an important development of basic economic infrastructure, both for Thailand and the cooperating nations of the region; this proposed canal should also be seen as a keystone, around which might be constructed a healthy and balanced development of needed basic infrastructure in a more general way."

Speaking on Aug. 7, 2015, LaRouche recalled this process, and noted: "Only stupidity by governments and other agencies has prevented these things from being accomplished long, long ago.... Look at the waste of time! All these things were ready and available to be done as major projects."

More than 30 years after LaRouche's remarks in Bangkok, with the BRICS and allied nations now moving in that direction, and under conditions of the disintegration of the British Empire's entire trans-Atlantic financial system, that potential can now be realized.

For Further Reading

• "Egypt Mobilizes To Build the New Suez Canal," by Dean Andromidas and Hussein Askary, *EIR*, Sept. 5, 2014.

• "Euphoric Egypt Steps Into the 21st Century," by Hussein Askary, *EIR*, March 27, 2015.

• "Nicaragua's Canal: The Maritime Silk Road Comes to the Americas," by Gretchen Small, *EIR*, January 9, 2015.

• "Nicaragua Canal: 'Great Project of Physical and Human Transformation,'" an interview with Dr. Telémaco Talavera, president of the Agrarian University of Nicaragua and spokesman for the Nicaragua Great Inter-Oceanic-Canal Commission, *EIR*, January 9, 2015.

• "China and the Coming Revolution in Global Cargo," by Dennis Small, *EIR*, January 9, 2015.

PRESIDENT EL-SISI:

New Suez Canal Is Egypt's 'Gift for Humanity'

At the Aug. 6 ceremony in Ismailia opening the New Suez Canal, Egyptian President Abdel Fattah el-Sisi delivered a historic address, which we excerpt below, as published by the Egyptian State Information Service:

"With God's blessings, I, Abdel-Fattah el-Sisi, President of Egypt, give permission for the operation of the New Suez Canal.... Within one year, Egyptians exerted a great effort to offer to the world and to Egypt a gift for humanity, for development, for building and for construction....

"Egypt is a great country and has a civilization of 7,000 years. I want to say that Egypt throughout these years has provided values, principles and ethics, which were in harmony with the heavenly religions and did not contradict them. Today, Egypt is offering a new gift for humanity," el-Sisi said, pointing out that that gift is no greater than what the ancient Egyptians proffered, but it was accomplished in only one year.

"Work did not take place in normal circumstances, and these circumstances still exist, and we are fighting them and we will defeat them. Evil was trying to harm Egypt and the Egyptians, and to halt its development.

"Egypt during this year stood against the most dangerous terrorist threat that would burn the world if it could.... It was the Egyptians who confronted these thoughts, to show the tolerance and the real image of Islam and Muslims. History will record that Egypt took on its shoulders the responsibility for renewing the religious discourse to make it consistent with the modern age."

El-Sisi called these groups "the groups of evil," who "are trying to harm Egypt and Egyptians and hinder the country's march of progress....

"The New Suez Canal is one step of thousands of

Xinhua/MENA

President el-Sisi addresses the ceremony unveiling the New Suez Canal, in Ismailia, Egypt, August 6.

steps which we all are required to take," he said, and that no one can harm the Egyptian people as long as they are one hand and united.

"We, the Egyptians, promised the world to provide the gift, and we have kept our promise and accomplished the project in a record time," he said.

He continued, "The launch of navigation in the new waterway that was accomplished in a record time surpasses the achievement of economic or political goals, as it highlights a humane goal that achieves dignity, justice and stability to the Egyptian people in a modern and democratic country."

"The development of the canal region is aimed at establishing a global economic zone which comprises a number of ports, new cities, and logistics and trade centers which will help achieve higher rates of trade exchange between Egypt and the whole world."

El-Sisi also outlined that a package of projects has been launched to establish a national road network, reclaim one million feddans of land, and establish new cities.

"I assure you that the Egyptian state is determined to move forward with social and political reform to achieve the aspirations of its sons," he told his fellow Egyptians.

Grant and Sherman On the Nile

by Jeffrey Steinberg

Aug. 11—From 1869-1883, a group of 50 American military officers, veterans of the Union and Confederate armies of the Civil War, were voluntarily dispatched to Egypt to help establish a national army and a military training program, based on the model of West Point. Members of the American team developed coastal defenses, conducted missions of exploration throughout the Horn of Africa, built a formidable Egyptian army and navy, and established an educational system for the children of the Egyptian armed forces.

The "Americans on the Nile" project was launched by the enlightened Khedive of Egypt, the administrator for the Ottoman Empire, Ismael Pasha. Ismael approached Thaddeus Mott, a West Point graduate then serving in the Ottoman Army after having fought with the Union Army in the Civil War. The son of a prominent physician and an anthropologist himself, Mott received permission from President Ulysses S. Grant's Army Chief of Staff, Gen. William Tecumseh Sherman, to recruit the team of American officers. Mott traveled in 1869 to Egypt, accompanied by Gen. Charles Pomeroy Stone and Gen. Henry H. Sibley. Stone would remain in Egypt through 1883, and became the Chief of Staff to Khedive Ismael Pasha.

The American mission was fiercely opposed by the British and the French, who were as adamantly opposed to Egyptian independence and sovereignty as the Ottomans, whose grip on Egypt had already been weakened by the Anglo-French machinations. The feeling was mutual, as reflected in the memoirs of Gen. William Wing Loring, a prominent member of the mission, from his decade in Egypt. Loring wrote a stinging denunciation of the Anglo-French efforts to loot Egypt, based on the debt that had been incurred through the building of the Suez Canal.

By 1878, the British-French combination conducted a coup in Egypt. They forced the abdication of Ismael Pasha, as a precondition for a debt restructuring. British and French officials were installed as heads of the Finance Ministry and other key posts. The first demand of the Anglo-French debt-holders was the dismantling of the American-built Egyptian Army and Navy. Soon, 80% of the armed forces were shut down, and all but one of the remaining American officers—Gen. Stone—were sent home.

The impact of the American officers on the future of Egypt, however, was not to be so easily wiped out. Under American commanders, including Gen. Charles Chaille-Long and Major James M. Morgan, major explorations were conducted into present-day Uganda, Democratic Republic of Congo, and Sudan. Major lakes and rivers, part of the Nile River tributaries system, were mapped for the first time, and the Mediterranean coastal defense were established that would serve Egypt in the future. Most importantly, the Egyptian equivalent of West Point was firmly established, along with a high-quality educational system for the children of the Egyptian military. In effect, a seed was planted that would be an essential feature of the Egyptian republican revolution of 1919. Many of the leaders of that independence movement were themselves either veterans of the American military program or children of those Egyptian officers. The full account of the American hand in Egypt's future is yet to be written; however, the fact that, to this day, the Egyptian armed forces are seen as the backbone of any patriotic movement, speaks volumes about the long-term impact of the American mission.

The American deployments to Egypt were fully blessed by the Grant Administration. In 1872, Gen. Sherman paid a visit to the Americans in Egypt; in 1878, former President Grant, as part of his world tour, also visited the Americans serving the Khedive. Grant would write, at the time, that he marveled at the Egyptian history and considered it one of the highpoints of his entire world expedition.

The Americans who served in Egypt, in some instances, went on to great achievements in other parts of the world. William McEntyre Dye, one of the American officers on the Nile, went in 1888 to Korea, where he served as chief military advisor to the government, on the personal recommendation of Gen. Philip Sheridan. Confederate Army Engineer Samuel Henry Lockett, who organized the coastal defenses of Vicksburg, then went to Egypt, and later went to Chile, where he supervised railroad construction to the end of his life. Before moving to Chile, Lockett served under Gen. Stone in the construction of Liberty Island, where the Statue of Liberty was placed.

New Objectives On a Global Scale

Extracts from Lyndon LaRouche's Aug. 8 Dialogue with the Manhattan Project.

Dennis Speed: My name is Dennis Speed, and on behalf of the LaRouche Political Action Committee, I want to welcome you to our ongoing dialogue of the Manhattan Project with Lyndon LaRouche. We're in the midst of a mobilization which particularly kicked in after August 6, the 70th anniversary of the bombing of Hiroshima, although Mr. La-Rouche had called it much earlier. And in this mobilization, we've been making a very specific point: that Hillary Clinton needs to do something for humanity, and the United States, and that is, that we need her, and we need others, to take action to make sure that Barack Obama is as rapidly and efficiently removed from the power of the Presidency.

This is very important because we have been in this discussion, and this discussion has begun to progress. Mr. La-Rouche will give an opening statement, and it will be followed by questions. I believe that people who've been here know, just come to the microphone and ask your question. So, Lyn, floor's open.

Lyndon LaRouche: Good to hear from you again, and we shall, without looking too much on me at this point, let's get the thing started. That we are presently faced with a crisis of the United States, and of many other parts of the world as well. We're threatened with a great rate of death, should it happen, if Obama continues to remain in the Presidency. Because his intention is to launch thermonuclear war on a global scale. That's his intention. He's already been moving in that direc-

> Now we get a new chance, to do what should have been the case, in our nation, in our economy. This time, we have a chance to bring it back.

tion, and therefore our question is: How do we get rid of *him*, in order to free the people of the United States from the great terror that Obama's present policy threatens to most of the human species as a whole?

So, this is the crucial issue and this is the thing to be kept in mind. This issue. Because that's the point. And what people will ask questions about here, will obviously be relevant, implicitly, to answering, implicitly, also, the questions which the citizens who step forward to raise a question, will help us to see more clearly.

Q: Good afternoon, Mr. LaRouche. How are you?

LaRouche: I'm not too bad for an old geezer. Go ahead.

Q: We're really glad to be here right now. My question is kind of an elementary one, and I just wanted to kind of get your ideas on this particular issue. We talk about the Guns of August. And for everyone here, I'd like you to just give us an idea of what is actually meant by the "Guns of August," and how that title ties into what we're talking about on a large scale today?

It Depends on Us

LaRouche: You should remember, even if you didn't know it as such, what happened in the course of history, beginning with the last decade before the new century came into being, that is the Twentieth Century; and at that point, what was called the Guns of August, which meant that a series of steps of warfare, had been going along from 1890 to about the beginning of the next century. And what this represents was the march of mankind from the beginning of the Twentieth Century, into what quickly became World War I.

And we're now faced with a challenge that a new world war, like so many other preceding world wars, is now come to depend on *us*. Because what Obama has done, President Obama has done, has brought the world up to a threat of thermonuclear war. Now, if that war, and that threat, were to be executed, there would probably be nobody left, no human beings alive on this planet. So, therefore, it's important that Obama be removed from the Presidency, in order to secure the human species.

We do not have to go to thermonuclear war. The world does not need thermonuclear war. Obama wants thermonuclear war. He's made it very clear. Our argument is: Obama should be removed from office *now*, in order to prevent him from launching thermonuclear war. And the danger of that launching is right now. It comes right in the person of Obama. Obama is on the edge of pushing over a process which would cause a thermonuclear war, worldwide.

What does that mean? That means that the conflict today is considered in terms of two points of reference: one is Obama, what his intention is. His intention is to launch thermonuclear war throughout most of the world. That's what the intention is. What's the alternative? Well, getting rid of Obama, and going back to the standards of the President of the United States, as we had experienced that, for example, with a great President, Kennedy, who, in his time, prevented the occasion of a killing thermonuclear war between Russia and the United States.

And so the time has come for two things: First, prevent this war that Obama is trying to bring on, and do it soon. Secondly, instead of having a thermonuclear war, we have to begin to organize cooperation among the major and other nations of the planet as a whole. We must go ahead, and understand what mankind is. Mankind is not an animal. No animal can invent the future. Only mankind, in the form of science, for example, can create the future. Mankind is a creature who lives on creating the future for mankind. And that's what we must achieve.

Wall Street Is Bankrupt

Q: I am R— from Bergen County, New Jersey, and this question is closer to the Glass-Steagall issue. Last week, in the *Wall Street Journal*, there is a gentleman by the name of Ken Griffin, who is a head of a hedge

> Our argument is: Obama should be removed from office now, in order to prevent him from launching thermonuclear war. . . . What's the alternative? Well, . . . going back to the standards of the President of the United States, as we had experienced that, for example, with a great President, Kennedy, who, in his time, prevented the occasion of a killing thermonuclear war between Russia and the United States.

NASA

President John F. Kennedy addresses Rice University on his program to send a man to the Moon, on September 12, 1962.

fund called Citadel Investments, and he was being interviewed, and he came up with what I found to be very intriguing, interesting statement that I think is a summary of a certain attitude among the Wall Street entity. His statement was, in talking to the type of business hedge funds are engaged in: We don't manufacture cars, we manufacture money. [LaRouche laughs]

So, my question is—I mean, this struck me as a pinnacle of monetarism, as a way of life; it just sums it up very well. The belief in money alone as a source of value. Could you comment?

So anyway, my question is: Can you comment on more of the morality aspects of monetarism, and how it

> Wall Street has to be cancelled. Every penny of Wall Street assets should be wiped off the books! And then, what we would do is create a Franklin Roosevelt-type of measure, a credit system to help in creating a program of employment, which will reconstruct the nation of the United States as a whole.

LaRouche PAC

LaRouche's Political Action Committee rallies at Federal Hall in Manhattan, March 19, 2015.

kind of poisons people's attitude; it has a very negative moral implication?

LaRouche: Put him back on the screen, now. I have more to say. I want to look at him, in order to address him.

OK, what you pose is very complicated—in some degree—question. And it needs a full explanation. These are very important things, because you've raised certain questions, which I do not agree with, but I think you will accept it quickly, when I identify these measures; and I think it important, before this audience, that they have a chance to understand exactly what I'm talking about, and what he's talking about at the same time. Because, I think we converge, in terms of our general intention. And I'm ready to take it on.

What Glass-Steagall Means

Now, look: There are many assumptions in what you say which are fair assumptions, but they're not necessarily accurate. Let me explain: The issue here is that Wall Street is totally bankrupt; it is *hopelessly bankrupt*; there's nothing that can save Wall Street.

The question is, since Wall Street is going to go

bankrupt anyway, put it in bankruptcy, but you have to have a step. Instead of having a monetarist conception of the U.S. economy, you have to have a human conception of what the economy is. That means that we want to have productive employment throughout our population, as a mode of existence, and that the government of the United States shall cancel everything except Glass-Steagall, and oppose anything that is not Glass-Steagall. And the United States government now has to create—after dumping these banking interests, which must be *cancelled, plain cancelled*. They are worthless, and therefore you cannot argue, that the people of the United States have to pay a bill for a worthless value, or less than worthless value.

So, therefore, that has to be done, which means that an extended application of Glass-Steagall, must replace *entirely* the Wall Street system. In other words, the Wall Street system must be put into the garbage pail. The people who go bankrupt, all right, let them go bankrupt and let them stay bankrupt if they want to.

But we must take steps to provide the people of the United States with the means, monetary means, of reconstructing the ability of the people of the United States, to be able to be employed in ways which are reasonable for the service of the United States, as such. And we would assume that everything we would do, under those kinds of conditions would be consistent with a generous attitude toward the other nations of the planet.

But the United States has to be defended! Wall Street has to be cancelled. *Every penny* of Wall Street assets should be wiped off the books! And then, what we would do is create a Franklin Roosevelt-type of measure, a credit system to help in creating a program of employment, which will reconstruct the nation of the United States as a whole.

Cancel Wall Street

That is a simple way of dealing with this. That is the fact! That's what must be done. Anything that is not doing that, is absolutely wrong and is a threat to the existence, of the citizens of the United States.

Thank you very much for sticking on, on this thing, but I wanted this thing to be explained clearly.

Q: I had another question which is a slightly different topic. That when I talk to people, I don't talk to a huge number of Americans, but, when I do talk to them, it seems like sometimes that they're from outer space. I don't know where they're coming from, to be euphemistic, to be kind. My question is, do you think that Americans now, are more complacent that the Germans were in the 1930s? Can we call the U.S. in its current state, "fascism"?

LaRouche: No. It could be considered that, but I don't think we should be hanging around, waiting for that to happen! What we should do is simply cancel Wall Street. Cancel Wall Street! Because the United States must create a fund for productive purposes. We must rebuild our economy! The people of the United States are suffering greatly from the conditions of life today. We must take steps which would do mainly one thing, even from the beginning: We're not going to wait until success blossoms above us. We are going to make it clear, to the major part of the population as a whole, that we in the United States are committed to *cancel* the Wall Street system, and come up with a contrary system, which is the Franklin Roosevelt principle; same thing.

But we have a much more urgent problem than Franklin Roosevelt had to face, because the murderous characteristics are much more important today, than they ever were under Franklin Roosevelt.

However, once Franklin Roosevelt died—and I have a very special attachment to Franklin Roosevelt; but, when he died, what happened was that his death allowed scoundrels of various types to take over through the Truman Administration. And we never really recovered from that. We've gone generally sliding down, more poorly and more poorly ever, ever since President Roosevelt died.

And so, the point is, we have a big job: we have to take the same kind of program that President Franklin Roosevelt proposed, to create that kind of a credit system. And we have to get our people to work in forms of employment, which are suitable to the dignity of American labor, and the families of those people.

And that's my summation of my view on this thing.

This Race Thing Is Crazy

Q: Good afternoon. My name is Miss J—. The reason why I'm up here is because I want to know—I have a couple of questions: Why is it that we blame President Barack Obama for the state that the U.S. is in, when he's not the only one to blame?

LaRouche: Because Obama is not a black person. That's got to be eliminated. I don't care what the color of his skin is, he's a bad person! And therefore he does nothing but evil. So therefore we don't need to make him a hero. He's not a hero. We've got plenty of people with perfectly black skins, who are much more preferable for doing this kind of job. And the time has come to break with it.

I mean, this race thing is crazy. There is no difference among the human race—*none*! There is no moral difference. Except that some people get kicked, and some people get less kicked. And the point is, yes, we have to clean this mess up. The South—you know, the third President of the United States was an evil man, and he created the slavery system in his tenure. And they continued to follow that bastard, through about three more Presidencies.

So yes, the United States has committed a permanent crime, against those who were called slaves, and those who were slaves in effect. And the racialist character of this thing is the greatest abomination that the United States has ever suffered. And that has to be ended. We cannot have any discrimination in terms of race or anything like that! We cannot have it. Look, we've got a lot of yellow people, so-called—Chinese. The largest single unit of population on the entire planet, is yellow. And you want to go down through all the shadings of color of skin? *Skin color has nothing to do with human reality!* [applause]

Q: My next question is, how do you plan on getting the President out of office?

LaRouche: By impeaching him, throwing him out of office.

Q: Okay, I know that the impeachment process has been underway for over a year, so I don't know at what timeframe do you think—

LaRouche: We have to be more quick. [In 1967], we had a new law put on the books concerning the Presidency. And under the influence of that law, we threw a rotten President out of office, and we did it on a short notice. That law still exists. Obama is a suitable target for that law. Throw him out of office. Do it tomorrow morning, or the day after tomorrow. Do it soon. He's got to be thrown out of office, for the sake of the human species in general. Remember, what Obama represents,— Obama has built up a warfare policy, which threatens the entire planet, the entire human population of the planet. We have to take him out of office. Now, the idea of shooting him is not a good idea; morally it's a bad idea. As a criminal, he should stay safe and alive in prison.

Congress Is Sleepwalking

And therefore, the point is, get this guy out of there. We don't need him, we don't want him; human beings don't want him. He's an animal, he's not really a human being. He's vicious, he's a vicious character! Look, how many people do you think he killed, offhand on his own right? There was no legality to that, there was no justice in that! He's a murderer! A public murderer. He murders all throughout the world; he organizes mass murder, throughout parts of the world in general. We don't *need* this guy!

The sooner we throw him out of office under the provision of the Constitution which now obtains, the better human beings' life will be.

Q: Good afternoon, Lyn; it's B— from New Jersey. In the last few weeks, I know there's been a major mobilization to break the sleepwalking going on particularly among Congress, in which we're trying to do that through interventions into the press, the news, the radios. I myself have been moving to get meetings with Congressional staff. In fact, I had a direct call from a congressman two days ago in answer to one of my requests, and arranged a meeting coming up the early part of this coming week.

But also, before Obama made this shift in Syria, I'd been writing to the newspapers, and I'd just like to give people a sense of potentially the way they can possibly intervene using Letters to the Editor. It goes:

"Hillary Clinton Must Come Clean on Benghazi Now"

"Former Secretary of State Clinton, and her chief of staff Cheryl Mills, faced with having to give sworn testimony before Congress in October, on events during, before, and after the Benghazi attack, should instead do so, publicly, now. The weight of existing public evidence and prepared under-oath questions shows she and other government officials were pressured by Obama to lie about that, then. Events now unfolding, require the truth. Although this will mean the end of her political aspirations, it could stop Obama, who, now unfettered by a recess Congress, is prepared to star a serial like 'I Have Decided' confrontation with Russia. Out-of-the-blue added sanctions, confirmation of his

new Chairman of the Joint Chiefs of Staff, who has declared Russia our greatest threat, and added movement of naval and ground-based ABM and other conventional assets, right to the borders of Russia itself, have prompted the highest-level warnings from the Russia government, diplomatic and military officials.

"This exact type of confluence of events is exactly why, after President Eisenhower's warning of a military-industrial complex, Kennedy had his staff reading *The Guns of August*.

"Clinton's considerations must now rise above all others, to effect a change, whose implication by exposing Obama, could sway events with national and global outcomes. Russia Duma Chairman Sergei Naryshkin gave a lengthy interview on July 30th in which he warned that a Third World War would be mankind's end." [as read]

And I think that everyone in this listening audience, and whoever we can get to, should be making that point clear to the Congress.

LaRouche: That's exactly my point. I agree with you totally on the whole thing.

Follow Roosevelt's Policy

Q: Good afternoon, nice to see you. I'm R— from Brooklyn. I was on two rallies this week and I noticed that the educational system has so indoctrinated people, that when we say Obama is starting World War III or beginning World War III, people have no frame of reference, to comprehend what we are trying say. And would you suggest a tactic we could break down this indoctrination?

LaRouche: Well, that's what I'm occupied with chiefly right now. I'm concerned essentially of course with the immediacy of the threat of thermonuclear war, which is embodied in the intention of Obama. That's the first issue.

The second issue of leadership, is what are we going to do, in order to shut down Wall Street? Because Wall Street is totally bankrupt; it's hopelessly bankrupt. I can never be reconstructed. There's no value in it any more. And the problem is, what we have to do, is we have cancel the worthless assets of Wall Street: Just shut it down. Forget it, it's a lost cause.

What we have to do instead, is follow Franklin Roosevelt's policy, during the 1930s. What we have to do is create a provision for circulation of legitimate, Federal government sources of wealth, that is economy, and we must do this with the idea, that for all the major parts of the U.S. population which are virtually ruined, and in a hopeless situation, we have to create a fund of the type Franklin Roosevelt used for the 1930s. We have to use that fund and allocate it, in order to create the kinds of welfare benefits, and health care, and productivity which Franklin Roosevelt did during his terms of office as President. That model, which has been tested already, is the sufficient law to the do the job that has to be done in developing the strength of our economy, developing the benefits of our people, and that's all it takes.

Bring back Franklin Roosevelt's approach to crisis by that method, the same method he used, but we have to apply it in more modern terms, and we have to rehabilitate citizens who are almost without hope. Increasingly, under Obama, the rate of acceleration of loss of wealth, of loss of the chance of life itself, has destroyed things so badly, that only a desperate measure, will work, like throwing him out of office and putting through a Franklin Delano Roosevelt-type of recovery program, using the power to create the currency, in order to provide the means for health and for employment-improvement among our citizens, and giving us a modern economy as well. That is what we must do as a minimal standard for this occasion right now. It can be done. There's no difficulty, there's no excuse, which will justify not doing it.

Mankind Is Not an Animal

Q: Hi, my name is A—. You sort of answered my question, it's more so on the economy, but maybe you can say a little bit more on, being a physical economist yourself, you know, today, most of the world is moving towards—at least away from a monetarist, mathematical economy, and there's a real transformation going on in most of the planet, you know, with this BRICS global phenomenon going on. And it's through this transformation that people, even in the transformation in their minds, like what a real economy actually is and what it involves. And it seems like your idea of physical economy sort of touches upon every aspect of human life. You can say more on that.

But just on the BRICS and what happened in Egypt recently, I think that's a transformation going on, that

> What we have to do instead, is follow Franklin Roosevelt's policy, during the 1930s. What we have to do is create a provision for circulation of legitimate, Federal government sources of wealth, that is economy, and we must do this with the idea, that for all the major parts of the U.S. population which are virtually ruined, and in a hopeless situation, we have to create a fund of the type Franklin Roosevelt used for the 1930s.

EIRNS/Stuart Lewis

A street scene in the U.S. Capital, December 2010.

the BRICS has actually materialized; it's a real physical impact taking place, on the planet right now. And it's just changing—it sort of embodies your idea of physical economics. Maybe you can say more on that?

LaRouche: Yeah, well, that's the point. What we have to understand about the nature of mankind, is a way of addressing what you have said, just now. The point is that mankind is not an animal: First fact. Mankind is not an animal. Mankind cannot be identified by any name of animal. Why? Because the human being, in its normal state, mankind, is always going to higher levels of discovery, in space, in everything else. And mankind's creative powers are unique to mankind; it's expressed often as scientific advances, but there are other things as well. And the progress of mankind, the development of progress, the development of the spirit, of the mind, of the skills of mankind, that's the issue.

Because, what's the meaning of all this? Mankind dies, people die. Is that the end of the meaning of their life? It should not be; for me it is not. Because what happens is, the normal course of life of mankind, is dif-

So therefore, all of this is available to us. It's available to us, through the realization of what we call scientific discovery; scientific principles which carry man to a power over nature, which is beyond anything mankind had experienced previously. And the proper motive of mankind is that mankind must say to their children, "You," the children, "will be empowered to discover principles of nature and a power of nature which earlier generations were not capable of achieving."

NASA

Astronaut David A. Wolf on a space walk off the International Space Station, October 2002.

ferent generations, successive generations of people acquire superior qualities of productivity at a higher level of productivity, at a higher level of skill, mastery of new skills that mankind had not known before. So mankind's role is, yes, we're all going to die in due course, or maybe a little earlier than due course in many times. But the point is, mankind is a creature of the future. No animal is a creature of the future, only mankind, and the purpose is that mankind must become better, and stronger, and richer in terms of effect with successive generations.

An Immortal Species

The greatest period of renaissances in human history, have been periods of great originality in achieving new skills, new principles of knowledge. And that's what makes mankind. So the devotion has to be of the development of mankind, to rise to higher degrees of power, to discoveries of scientific powers which mankind has known before, and to bring those forces to bear; because now, mankind is not just on Earth, you know; with Kepler's arrival we already had the Solar System. Kepler exposed the Solar System's existence to us. And now we're in a higher system, which is called the Galactic System, and most of the water in the system that our life depends upon, is based on the Galaxy, not on the Earth's water system. Earth's water system is a minor part of the whole water system of the Galactic System.

So therefore, all of this is available to us. It's available to us, through the realization of what we call scientific discovery; scientific principles which carry man to a power over nature, which is beyond anything mankind had experienced previously. And the proper motive of mankind is that mankind must say to their children, "You," the children, "will be empowered to discover principles of nature and a power of nature which earlier generations were not capable of achieving."

And that's the attitude on which we have to operate. That's the conception of *man, mankind*. And thus mankind is an immortal species in this respect. Mankind may die, but when mankind is productive, mankind before dying, contributes something, with which the next coming generations will achieve a higher rate of development of the human species than the previous ones. And the fact is that people used to think that way. They'd say, "What is life all about?" The immigrants used to talk about that. People who came as immigrants into the United States. And they would think about, "Things are tough for us right now. We're immigrants. We don't have the access, we don't have the right accents and so forth, therefore we have to accept a poorer position than most of the native Americans of that time."

Moral Principle of Mankind

But the point of the purpose was, well so what? You have a family, your family is integrated into the United States by immigration in many cases, and therefore you have a right to partake, through your children, a right to get the kind of education, the knowledge, the opportunities which earlier populations had achieved inside the United States. And in turn we have to give them to all the people of the United States together, both immigrants, and those who have been, shall we say, regular citizens.

We have to make each generation of humanity more meaningful than what the earlier generation had been capable of doing. And it's that concept of progress, which is not just physical progress; it's the progress of the human mind, and the human mind's ability to make discoveries which mankind of the earlier times, had not been able to do.

So what you get is a principle of triumph. Mankind is a constant principle of triumph. Mankind must always reach to higher levels of achievement, for the future of mankind, at each turn. And that is the moral principle on which we should base all our assumptions, all our doctrines. That mankind is the perfect case, the perfect growth which can do everything that no animal could ever have achieved.

Q: Good afternoon Mr. LaRouche. My name is A——. Obama is crazy and creating situations that could easily become a thermonuclear war, either by intent or by accident. Since his actions are insane, doesn't he qualify for removal as of the Twenty-Fifth Amendment, or indictment under the Nuremberg World Court? Could the United Nations bring Obama up on charges before the war becomes nuclear?

LaRouche: Yeah. Well the purpose of this thing is obvious, that's the nature, of which we in the United States should have adopted. I don't think we always did adopt it.

But the recognition that we are all going to die; everybody dies eventually. The question is, what is the outcome of the life of the person who dies? And the person who creates a generation, builds up a generation, to a higher level than they themselves had achieved, is the great heroic statement.

Twenty-Fifth Amendment

What is the definition of human immortality? It's the realization of creativity on behalf of mankind's mission, which always leads to a higher and better form of expression of human achievement than before. This was true in the characteristic of the Renaissance, for example the medieval Renaissance, so called, was the same thing. The idea of the permanent Renaissance, that mankind should always rise to a higher level of achievement, moral achievement, practical achievement, than the generation before, as an average of the situation.

Mankind thus progresses, as no animal can progress. No animal can choose a superiority over man, because mankind is the highest level. And therefore the population of a nation must *progress*, in the service of the Almighty, in the end.

Q: Can Obama be brought up on charges, before it becomes nuclear?

Speed: Lyn, he's asking whether Obama can be brought up on charges by the 25th Amendment [crosstalk]

LaRouche: Yes he can, in the period of the 1960s and '70s there was—a bill was put through which dumped a President out of office in midterm. And right now, and any time you want to, there is a statutory provision, under the Constitution of the United States presently, that any President, such as, for example, Obama, who's no damn good, shall we say, and therefore can be dumped out of office suddenly, by the proper means of our Constitution. And that should happen.

Q: Hi Lyn, this is A——. I wanted to, in the context of the Manhattan Project as it were, talk about music insofar as, early on in the process as I am, and being a part of the chorus, and even my participation has been somewhat limited, the idea is finally starting to register in my mind; because of the challenges that the work requires, the fears, one has to either decide to run away from it and not come back, or return and work through the tensions that are there. And I mean it's all very friendly, but those things exist. And I find it very challenging, but I'm beginning to get the understanding that if you can work through this with a group of people, and develop yourself, then the question of confronting your fellow citizen on the threat of thermonuclear war becomes less fearful. [LaRouche laughs.] You're facing your own fears.

A Miracle Event

So it's early on, but it never really made sense, I just went to sing; but the thing is starting to come together. And then the idea of doing what we need to do, which seemed impossible, begins to seem more possible to me now. So I just wanted to share that and get something

The point is that the importance of music is a moral one, in a very special kind of way. It's a moral force which leads to improvements in all the qualities of the human individual. And when they're deprived of that, it's like bad education, bad schooling, which destroys the morality and destroys the rights, of the citizen,—the child and the citizen in general,—and therefore there's a kind of a sacred implication of the sort of magic which is expressed by Classical artistic composition as such.

Facebook page of Lynn Yen

A chorus rehearsal in Brooklyn, New York, in September 2012, sponsored by Lynn Yen's Foundation for the Revival of Classical Culture.

back from you on that.

LaRouche: Okay, well the point is, is that the composition of progress, and composition of musical composition, Classical musical composition is a miracle event, in the sense of ordinary opinion. Because creativity, true creativity in music, for example, depends upon a development of the idea of music, which is always perfect. That as it goes ahead, the general history, the course of history from Bach, on to the present time, there has always been a current of progress up until the beginning of the Twentieth Century.

At that point we had a general degeneration in the quality, intellectual quality and moral quality of music. That is the form of music that in the later generation, as of the Twentieth Century, what was generally provoked prominently, was a degenerating process in terms of music.

Now the significance of that for music is, that the effect is, that bad music, that is poor music, that is, music that is not fit for mankind, shall we say, has created a degeneration of everything in terms of the moral aspects of human life over the course of the Twentieth Century and beyond. It became more and more acute, particularly after Franklin Roosevelt died. But then, there were heroes who stood up again, like Eisenhower, for example, stood upm was one of those heroes, and they represented a defense of the principles of United States where certain Presidents of the United States had failed, brutally.

The point is that the importance of music is a moral one, in a very special kind of way. It's a moral force which leads to improvements in all the qualities of the human individual. And when they're deprived of that, it's like bad education, bad schooling, which destroys the morality and destroys the rights, of the citizen,—the child and the citizen in general,—and therefore there's a kind of a sacred implication of the sort of magic which is expressed by Classical artistic composition as such. And this, as through Brahms, for example, and through Furt-wängler, for example, who are leading examples of this thing, that approach to music is not a mechanical one, is not a practical one. It's a moral principle, that mankind's ability to think in terms of what we call music, rises and lifts mankind upward; whereas bad music, or junk music destroys the creative powers and moral powers of the population. So there needs to be a moral drive which compels people to find a greater virtue in their life than before.

Jesu, Meine Freude

Q: Hi Lyn, this is D—. I was reflecting on the development of our force here in Manhattan, as the germ of the national Center of this organization, and at this moment in our community chorus in New York City, and also in our New Jersey chorus, we're working on *Jesu, meine Freude* by Bach. And my question to you is, I know that before I became a member of this organization, the youth movement that you created did a lot of work on this piece. And so in a sense, I think it's very fitting that as this chorus comes together right now, this is what we're working on. And my question is, what is the significance of *Jesu, meine Freude*?

LaRouche: It's obviously topical. But what it represents is a principle, in which people can affirm a relationship with the process of life and death combined. In other words, what is the meaning of *Jesu, meine Freude*? It represents the fact that mankind is living in a struggle, a struggle of life, and mankind has to find a standard of behavior, self-imposed behavior, which is in accord with what they believe to be the right means of bringing about progress into the future of mankind.

I mean, everything that is serious about religious belief, Christian religious belief in particular, is all based on that principle: The presumption is, everybody dies sooner or later. *But!* Some people actually advance, despite death, to a higher level of achievement, than they had represented even in their own lives. And that's the meaning, of *Jesu, meine Freude*.

Hillary Is a Failure

Q: Hi, my name is C— and thank you for having me. This is my first time here, and I find it very interesting. I love politics. My question is, if Hillary doesn't move forward, and I feel that she may not, if she's really concerned about being President; but if she doesn't, what can we do at the local level? I'm in local politics, and I'd like to know, what can we do at this level?

LaRouche: Well, I think what's going to happen, is, as of now, and what I can give you is only a qualified guess as to what the outcome would be. Hillary is a failure. She blew it, shall we say, in various ways, by keeping her mouth shut in one case, which really sunk her; and then she killed herself more by the things she did say, after the mess she made of not saying.

So she's finished, implicitly finished. And that's regrettable, because she at one point was a fairly, more than reasonable person. But she had a certain weakness, which is a, shall we say, a political problem.

But anyway, that's the nature of the problem, and there is a solution immediately, and the solution is, she should withdraw from office because she's going to be sinking deeper and deeper at an accelerating rate, in the competition for campaigns now. She's finished. But she can have a decent way out by admitting that she had lied, under pressure from the President, in what happened in North Africa; and that's clear, she committed a crime. She lied, under pressure of the President; well, the criminal is actually the President, Obama. He's the

criminal. So he should be put out of office, and we should have Hillary going into a different career, because she's not going to become President.

But then, we have to take this case and not leave it there, and say what is the standard? What is the standard of behavior which is required, by the citizen, when we enter into the idea of election campaigns? And there are certain standards which are implicit; they don't have to be detailed, they're implicit. And when they make the wrong move, as she has done, then she's going to take a back seat. But I'd be happy to see her still living, and I'm not sure that Obama will not kill her, because I know him.

Q: I agree with you. Any thoughts on the 2016 Presidential race right now?

LaRouche: Well, I can't draw a conclusion. I can draw a very good estimate. We have a couple of people who are, right now, already credible appellants for the Presidency, as opposed to things that I know aren't fit to run for the Presidency.

2016 Elections

But see, when I talk about President, I don't think about President, I think about the Presidential *system*. Because contrary to myth, it is not the President that defines the character of the administration; it's the combination of people, who are the combined forces of the Presiden*cy* as such, and if that combination of the right Presiden*cy* comes into place, then you will get a corresponding benefit in the next round of elections.

And that I think is the rough guess of what the best possibilities are. I think we have—O'Malley has obvious potential; some others have some significant potential. And I just think we're going to have to live it out: If you want to choose a good Presidential candidate, you better get in there and work with them. You have to make it a good Presidential system.

Q: I agree. Thank you so much.

Q: Hi how are you. My name is J—; I'm from China. My question is, how can you forecast the relationship between China and the U.S.A. in terms of politics, economic culture, and education?

LaRouche: Well, you just touched upon a very important issue, which is beyond the actual question that you're posing. Because what's happening, is, China of course is undergoing a great step of progress, under the present administration of China. This is good, very good. There are problems in China which are nuisance values, where you have a big speculative thing of some

When I talk about President, I don't think about President, I think about the Presidential system. Because contrary to myth, it is not the President that defines the character of the administration; it's the combination of people, who are the combined forces of the Presidency as such, and if that combination of the right Presidency comes into place, then you will get a corresponding benefit in the next round of elections.

creative commons/Ralph Alswang

Both Bernie Sanders (left) and Martin O'Malley (right) are stressing the need to return to Glass-Steagall in their campaigns for the Democratic Party nomination.

groups of people, who are placing in financial speculation.

But the China system is a very good system as it stands now; it's been a great improvement over what the deep potential of China has been for a very long period of time. And China has a great history, one of the greatest histories of any living nation. And they've gone through various ups and downs, and fights and quarrels, in certain factions inside among the Chinese population, or different parts of it.

The Chinese System

But in general, the present administration of China is a miracle of the century. It now is bringing India back to life; it hasn't been fully brought back to life, but it's going back to life. Take the whole region, like the new thing that just happened Egypt, the canal in Egypt. The canal in Egypt, has opened up the world so that you no longer have an Atlantic nation as opposed to an Asian nation. Everything's going to change suddenly as a result of what happened by the Egyptian change right now; everything's going to change—beautifully. Parts of things in the southern parts of the planet, different

parts of the planet, are going to improve as a result of this thing, given a chance.

So this is a great moment, and most of the problems we face are not really net disasters; they are challenges. And it's up to the people who have the opportunity to seek that kind of success, it's up to them to demonstrate their ability to seize upon the options that are presented to them; and the current China administration,—it's very well qualified in this respect, the achievements are very great.

We would wish that, for example, other parts of Asia would go the same way, for example, look at Japan. Japan, you know, coming out after the defeat of Japan in World War II, the unfortunate thing was that the President of the United States committed great crimes against the people of Japan, by dumping bombs, U.S. bombs, on two major cities of Japan. And the population of Japan, at that point was very peaceable; they decided they wanted there to be an end to the war that they'd gone through.

And during that period, my experience with Japan, was a very progressive process, and less so today. I think Japan has gone back a few steps in history. But at that time, Japan was, after coming out of a war, suffering the effect of a war, and of the President of the United States committing mass murder against people of Japan.

And that made everything worse in the area of Asia. I mean, the fact that the President of the United States dropped nuclear bombs on two cities of Japan, has left a mark which is still hitting Asia today, that example, that kind of situation.

So the point is, that we are in a period where I am optimistic about the future of China and therefore, there are problems, but these are problems which belong to China, not to outside busybodies. China is doing very well right now, and we should wish more nations had the same kind of success that China's had recently.

Q: How can you foresee the future of China? Like, the social system, will it change to a capitalist country, or do you see them as a communist country? Or. . . .

The Future of China

LaRouche: The class division among Chinese populations and culture—and that has been an off-and-on problem for a long time in China. I think the problem has been essentially been conquered as of now. I think that China is essentially in a very stable way, with some problems—but every nation has some problems. I think those problems can be solved.

And the cooperation of China with India, which is not always agreeable—I mean some of the people in India don't like China; they're jealous. But that's all right, it'll work out well.

And what's happened with the new canal by Egypt, has now changed the whole planet. There are no longer several oceans: There's now one ocean. And the Atlantic ocean and the Pacific Ocean are all opened up to the same thing. So we're coming to a new period, we're coming to where the nation-state is not as important as it used to be. The culture of a people is very important, because without the familiarity of their culture, they cannot really function perfectly. So therefore, while you have still, a distinction in language use and things like that, and cultural uses, in various parts of the world, in general, the entire planet should be becoming one nation. Not immediately, but in a process: Because mankind, is mankind. There is no difference between mankind and mankind!

But the question is how to make the practical expression of that unity be realized, as with the "win-win" concept in China, is an example of *exactly* that issue. And so, China plays a very leading role, in presenting that kind of influence throughout the Asian and other areas of the planet.

So this is good stuff, shall we say.

Q: Thank you very much.

What Roosevelt Did

Q: Yes, Mr. LaRouche, good to see you and I hope you live a long life, here. My question here, is, within the Federal government, there are, within my knowl-

> But the question is how to make the practical expression of that unity be realized, as with the "win-win" concept in China, is an example of exactly that issue. And so, China plays a very leading role, in presenting that kind of influence throughout the Asian and other areas of the planet.

Press Information Bureau of India

Indian Prime Minister Narendra Modi, and visiting Chinese President Xi Jinping, review plans for development in Gujarat, India in September 2014.

edge from the website reading, meaning that there are a few of them who are for Glass-Steagall. Now, I want to know, that being that this is an economy of money, what are they doing to fortify the Glass-Steagall Act, knowing that this is necessary because of the situation of the economy? And then, the second question is, the national bankers: Where are all these so-called national bankers? Are they afraid to step up to the plate to promote Glass-Steagall? What can we do to protect their interests? And then, the third question here is, being that the monarchy is a vicious group of people, and they do play psychological warfares; and they have families—they show this on the TV in the media, the birth of their new kids and the new monarchy coming in; would they be anarchistic to kill themselves and actually go for [world war], or is this all one big bluff? One big bluff to set—to make it appear that there's going to be a big war, so that the land-bridge and the Glass-Steagall issue will break down under pressure?

LaRouche: First of all, there is no chance that Wall Street is going to survive; there is no chance. Wall Street is hopelessly bankrupt! It's super-bankrupt! That it has no possible recovery options. The problem therefore, is

So therefore, the question is, what are we doing to steer the new direction that we think is necessary for mankind on a global scale? And therefore, we just take: OK, Franklin Roosevelt was right: We have to do the same kind of thing that he was trying to do with it, while he was still living, in order to develop the economy of the United States, with great degrees of progress.

President Franklin Roosevelt during his January 1943 visit to Morocco, where he discussed greening the deserts with Moroccan Sultan Mohammed V, seated to FDR's right.

since Wall Street is absolutely worthless, worse than worthless, it's a trash bin, and the stink from the trash bin is getting worse all the time. So therefore, what you have to do, you *cancel* Wall Street! The United States government cancels Wall Street, because it's in disorderly bankruptcy! It cannot be revived.

Now, what do we do? We go back to Franklin Roosevelt, we take the kind of disaster which occurred in the 1920s, we look at that, the Hoover thing. So Hoover sucks, but we don't use it otherwise except for vacuum cleaning.

So therefore, what Roosevelt did, was made a reform which was the foundation under Glass-Steagall, which enabled the United States to become a victorious nation, actually, in the course of World War II. We did it that way, why? Because Roosevelt made it possible, and organized it. We had general officers in charge of our command during my time in the military service, and they were heroes. They created geniuses in effect. And we went through a terrible war; many of

our people were killed. But that is what is true, that's what's good. We don't like to have those wars, we would like to get rid of those kinds of wars. But we think one of the best ways to do that, is to remove the British Empire, for example, and some other nuisances on the public account.

The Idea of Nations

And that we could bring nations together, because we're ready. You know, the old idea of the nation-state, is different than it was before. We used to have nations, "this nation is sacred, this nation is sacred," and so forth; well, it's not true any more. Because nations are more and more tending to mix in close cooperation with each other. Yet nations can still continue to function as they exist, but the closeness of cooperation among nations will be increased. And eventually, what we call "national systems," will probably disappear.

So therefore, the question is, what are we doing to steer the new direction that we think is necessary for mankind on a global scale? And therefore, we just take: OK, Franklin Roosevelt was right: We have to do the same kind of thing that he was trying to do with it, while he was still living, in order to develop, the economy of the United States, with great degrees of progress.

We went in the wrong direction, when the new President came into place.

And therefore right now, we have to say, no, we're not going to be chauvinistic nations; we're going to be nations which work together. We're going to be sovereign, but we're going to work together, we're going cooperate, we're going to solve problems commonly. And over the course of a century, we should be able to get the effect of a unified humanity on the planet. And we will not be limited to the planet. We will be going into space, as well.

Q: Thank you very much.

LaRouche: [Closing statement] Well, it's obvious that we're at precisely that point. What we have is an abused population of the labor force in the United States in general. The economy stinks. It's totally immoral the way it functions right now. The banking system is immoral and incompetent beyond belief. All we have to do, is make one single kind of law, based on the principle which is expressed by the Glass-Steagall law: Restore the Glass-Steagall law and understand what the power of the Glass-Steagall law can mean, not just what it *did* mean, but what it *can* mean if we know how to use it properly.

Our Objective

And the point is, what our objective is, is to get our citizens, first of all our children, our young children, our dependents; most of them are totally ignorant, of the *most essential facts of life*, that earlier generations like my own had already known as achievements. Most people in the United States today, have neither the experience or the opportunity of experience, nor an understanding of the principle, nor the skills involved, in order to make progress per capita throughout our society.

We are losing everything in terms of investment; all the skills that we had accumulated by a certain point are now *disappearing*, they're rotting away! And so therefore, what we have to do is recognize this fact, and by

supporting our people, *like a new Glass-Steagall law*, which wipes off *all* Wall Street investments in one stroke: *There's no value in that thing! Shut it down!*

We then turn around, in Franklin Roosevelt's neat trick, and he comes in with a system of creating money, to be used by the citizens and by producers, in order to make mankind in the United States, once again successful, and more successful than ever before. Now, he died unfortunately, and after he died, everything began to go rotten; the FBI took over and things like that. Corruption was tremendous.

But now the time has come for vengeance: The vengeance is simply achieving what we had been cheated of being able to do, earlier. Now we get a new chance, to do what should have been the case, in our nation, in our economy. This time, we have a chance to bring it back. [applause]

Speed: Well, that will not actually conclude our session of today, since everybody is going to be so agitated by what they've just heard, that I'm sure this is going to go on and on in their minds for many hours. But Lyn, I want to thank you for being with us, and we'll see you again next week.

LaRouche: OK! Have fun!